Healers on the Mountain

Healers on the Mountain

*Traditional Native American Stories
for Cleansing, Healing, Testing,
and Preserving the Old Ways*

Teresa Pijoan

August House Publishers, Inc.
LITTLE ROCK

Published by August House, Inc.,
P.O. Box 3223, Little Rock, Arkansas 72203,
501-372-5450.

Printed in the United States of America

10 9 8 7 6 5 4 3 2 1

LIBRARY OF CONGRESS CATALOGING-IN-PUBLICATION
DATA

Pijoan, Teresa
Healers on the mountain : traditional Native American stories for cleans-
ing, healing, testing, and preserving the old ways. p.   cm.
ISBN 0-87483-268-3 (alk. paper) : $19.00
ISBN 0-87483-269-1 (pbk.: alk. paper) : $10.00
1. Indians of North America—Religion and mythology. 2. Indians of
North America—Medicine.
I.Title.
E98.R3P54 1993
299'.72—dc20   93-29465

First Edition, 1993

Executive editor: Liz Parkhurst
Assistant editor: Jan Diemer
Design director: Ted Parkhurst
Cover design: Byron Taylor
Illustrations: Ray Bailey
Typography: Lettergraphics / Little Rock

This book is printed on archival-quality paper that meets the
guidelines for performance and durability of the Committee on
Production Guidelines for Book Longevity of the
Council on Library Resources.

AUGUST HOUSE, INC.   PUBLISHERS   LITTLE ROCK

To Lana M. Schaff—whose love for the written word has brought books to thousands of Southwest readers. Special thanks to:

Tom Baskett, Jr.
Jan Diemer
Judy and Richard Young
Alessandro Strong-Voice Salimbeni
Donna Jones Duran Omstead
Alex Key-Sen-Doh Apostolides
Nicole Kotcininako Pijoan
Claire Agoyo-povi Van Etten
Hannelore Hahn
With quiet love to Musa Barbara Pijoan

Preface

Healers on the Mountain is a book of detailed stories, or myths, showing the importance of spiritual harmony. Many popular stories these days are short, following plot lines and going directly to the point. But life is not like that—at least not in this author's view. Life is complex and erratic. It takes balance, understanding, and, most of all, *detail* to keep each one of us on our path. The following stories hold the truths of many and the sacred ways of those who have gone before. They are held here for you who wish to understand your path, your way, your harmony. May you always walk in beauty; and, as the Pueblo Indians say, may the pollen of life always be on your feet.

—Teresa Pijoan

Contents

Chants   91

Vision Quests   121

Healing Myths   175

Story Notes   211

Introduction

From the standpoint of health, the natural and cultural life of the Pueblo people has both advantages and problems. There is an abundance of clean, pure air and the potency of the sun. The wind cleans the land and keeps it cool. The aridity of the climate keeps one from sweating and quickly dries foul water. The thick-walled adobe homes stay cool in the summer and warm in the winter. On the other hand, people here face hard-blowing dust, drought, smoke-filled rooms, dysentery from bad water, and the problems of unknown diseases.

Yet "uncivilized" cultures have their remedies, known by the healers through dreams, myths, hallucinations, and traditions. Every group uses particular ceremonies and other means for diagnosis and remedy. These are performed for discovering specific remedies as well as for calling spirits that will help patients secure the proper action of the cures. In some cases, ghosts or spirits are summoned to tell of the illness. They are commanded, chanted to, and even threatened, to leave the body by the end of the ceremonial process.

Traditionally, medicine people have drunk special mixtures to give them strength for combating the ghosts or spirits. At some pueblos, medicine water, or *wopo* (*wo*=medicine; *po*=water), is prepared in connection with certain ceremonies.

Small quantities are collected from four sacred-water lakes; and to this is added water from the sky and water from below, obtained by digging a hole in the ground. These, then, are the six sources of water, and they are mixed in a *woposai* (medicine bowl) and used only at ceremony.

The fasting, feasting, dancing, meditation, and chanting by one or all are vital to opening the door of the ghost world or spirit land. Once the way is opened, the medicine people know how to use these apparitions to the patient's benefit.

Navaho ceremonies traditionally featured sacred reed sticks and prayer sticks. First, the people took two sheepskins and spread one upon the other before the song-priest. Upon these were laid a finely woven blanket, and on top of the blanket were placed strips of cotton running north and south. The healer took a large medicine bag, removed the proper reeds, and rubbed them against a polishing stone, holding the reeds high in the right hand and the stone in the left. He next rubbed the reeds with finely broken native tobacco, which was then divided into four pieces—each as long as the width of the first three fingers. Finally, he cut the reeds with a stone knife and gave each a sacred color. All the reeds had slender sticks of yucca that served as handles while they were being painted.

The first reed was painted blue and laid at the north end of the blanket. The second was painted black, the third blue, and the fourth black. Each blue reed got three dots representing eyes and a mouth, and two lines encircled the black reeds.

Next, four bits of soiled cotton cloth were placed in line to the east of the rug. The song-priest took from the medicine bag two feathers from the bluebird, placing them west of the cloth that lay at the rug's north end. He put two more of the same blue feathers below the second piece of cloth, two under the third, and two below the fourth, with all their tips facing east. Then he took the under-tail feather of an eagle, laid it on the two blue feathers at the north end of the rug, and placed a turkey's under-feather beside it. The feathers nearest each reed were decorated with beads, four tiny white shells, four pieces of abalone, and four pieces of turquoise.

Each reed was then packed with sacred tobacco, known as "sacred smoke." Next, the song-priest would take a sacred crystal, holding it so that it would catch the rays of sunlight in the ceremonial house, or *kiva.* He would direct the sun through the crystal to magnify its heat on the sacred reeds that were placed on the rug. This was how the sacred reed or the "sacred smokes" were lit. They were then smoked by the ceremonial priests.

Other methods were used to find the potency of remedies. For example, some people had knowledge of plants and how they cured. Plants of red juice acted on the blood; heart-shaped plants were used on the heart. All forms or resemblances of plants and animals had significance.

Answers came to the healer from training, dreams, traditional knowledge, and an ability to "see" the problem in the patient, along with the patient's perception of his own illness. Medicine people primarily had the power to diagnose and cure illnesses. Other people had power for other personal needs such as finding lost objects or ensuring success in hunting, war, love, and gambling. Most medicine people were older men, though there also were strong healing women, powerful in ceremonies and women's illnesses.

Usually, medicine people had medicine bags of sacred paraphernalia that included cattail pollen, paints, herbs, eagle feathers, quartz crystals, red ocher, and tobacco. Many wore red feathers with leather-thong necklaces of turquoise.

Medicine people were respected and feared, both in life and death, and they were given offerings. Their insignia and ritual tools—benches; *pah'hoos* (rattles and hand-held objects); dolls or idols or *Ka't'sinas;* quartz crystals; turquoise holy stones; and medicine bags, medicine sand, and medicine feathers—were considered just as sacred as the persons themselves. Items were, at times, given to others to hold and care for, and out of ultimate respect were considered sacred concepts of hope. They were alive, just like the persons holding them.

The power of the spirits used by medicine people came from animals, from the healers themselves, or from others who held the power and the knowledge as well. For instance, interpreters of dreams were considered seers or prophets, and they held great respect, too.

The treatment of disease itself depended much on the person *with* the disease. Different treatments were used for similar problems. To determine the best approach, the medicine person considered the character, personality, lifestyle, number of children, age, and capability of the patient.

In short, each person was different, and to believe that the same treatment could work on everyone was an untruth. Each patient held a different spirit, a different concept of belief, hope, and healing. Each had a different perception of his or her own unique disease. Each case, therefore, was unique and needed to be treated as such. The healing could only work when it affected the spirits of individuals, and that happened when patients felt the healers knew who they were and what they needed. The ones to be healed had to believe in their healers.

John Wesley Powell wrote in his Bureau of American Ethnology report of 1899, "In early civilization the chemical transmutation of things seems to excite the greatest wonder.... As poetry is now the fine art of allegory, so medicine is now the healing art whose lore is taught in allegory. When science comes, the art of medical remedies is emancipated from the art of alchemy, astrology is divorced from diagnosis, and the shaman becomes either a priest on the one hand or a physician on the other. Thus religion and medicine are divorced. But neither religion nor medicine is at once freed from superstition."

Medicine people practice to the point of curing themselves, their children, and their tribes, using their beliefs beyond any doubt. The Guiana Indians have illnesses that they know how to cure without going to a healer. However, if the home cures do not work, they go to another person until they find the healer who can help them. David Brinton wrote of Mayan priests: "As doctors, augurs, rain-makers, spell-binders, leaders of secret societies, and depositories of the tribal traditions and wisdom, their influence was generally powerful. Of course it was adverse to the Europeans, especially the missionaries, and also of course it was generally directed to their own interest or that of their class: but this is equally true of priestly power wherever it gains the ascendancy, and the injurious effect of the Indian shamans on their nations was not greater than has been in many instances that of the Christian priesthood in European Communities."

Dreams and Medicine

One split second of beauty can elevate the emotion to the highest of peaks. In a flash, there can be pain beyond compare—uncontrollable, unbearable, suffocating pain. Darkness can leave one in severe frustration, rejection and isolation. Deep fear can take over. Light, love, dreamy-soft emotion can bring relief and a feeling of union with self and pleasure.

Each silent conscious vision of sleep can cure or kill a disease or pain. Defeat or reward can become reality if the dream that feeds the spirit is bad or good. Healing the body can be done through the consciousness of dreams mixed with the hypnotic awareness of self-need. Each person has needs and intimate desires. Dreams done with positive impression can reroute the path of energy within the patient. Dreams that influence the waking person's vision of self and ability can heal the wounded body and allow the person to find a new whole and capable life path. Here then are the stories that perhaps were life dreams or were stories that brought about dreams that changed life.

1. Cherokee Dreams of Respect

When all of life spoke the same language, there was much happening everywhere. The animals spread and settled all over the earth. The birds spread and settled all over the earth. The snakes spread and settled all over the earth. The plants spread and settled all over the earth. The people spread and settled all over the earth and tried to take away land from the others. Man invented weapons to kill, took what was not rightfully his, and then fought to defend it.

The bears decided to meet and discuss what should be done with the people. They met under Kuwa-hi Mountain, also known as the Mulberry Place. Old White Bear Chief called the council together.

"There is always a way to find our defense," he said. "We must believe that we can do so. What is your complaint about the people?"

He heard each complaint and how man had killed friends and family for the meat, flesh, fur, and bones. White Bear Chief asked what the weapons were that men used to kill the bears. The bear people answered that they used bows and arrows.

"What are bows and arrows made of?" asked White Bear Chief.

"The bow is made of wood, and the bow string is made of our intestine," answered the bears.

White Bear Chief decided to make a bow and some arrows and use them on the men who were killing bear people.

They found the wood from a locust tree. One bear, who believed in the ability of his fellow bears, sacrificed himself for the purpose of protecting his family, and his intestine was used as the bow string. The arrows were made and the weapon was ready to be shot. The bear chosen to shoot had difficulty, for his claws got stuck in the bow string. They took a vote and decided to cut the claws off the bear.

White Bear Chief stopped them, saying, "Our claws give us the ability to climb trees, to protect ourselves against other animals, and to get our food. We cannot cut our claws. We must believe there is another way." They broke for a later discussion, but nothing was resolved.

The deer held a council with their chief. Little Deer. He spoke loudly at this meeting. He told them of his great powers and said that anyone shooting a deer for survival and food would be forgiven by saying a prayer at that time. Some hunters shot deer to feed their families, not just for the sake of killing. Hunters leaving corn meal in the dead animal's mouth for the soul of the deer to return would be blessed to hunt again. If the hunter did not say a prayer, however, Little Deer would give him rheumatism. The rheumatism would be debilitating, and the hunter would be unable to walk, much less hunt.

A deer runner was sent to warn the people. He told them that whenever a hunter shot a deer, Little Deer—swift as the spring wind—would come and listen. If Little Deer did not hear the hunter's prayer for pardon, the hunter would drop blood from his body on the ground as he carried the dead deer home, allowing the rheumatism to enter his body. When the hunter arrived at his home, he would be stricken with severe rheumatism, becoming a helpless cripple.

The fish and the snakes held council. It was decided that if someone killed a fish or a snake with no purpose in mind except to be mean, that person would suffer greatly. The senseless killing of fish and snakes had brought about much hopelessness, and some fish and snakes even died from fear and worry. The oldest snake spoke and told the younger snakes that hope had to be in each cell of their being, or there was no purpose for being alive. Fish and snakes were important to the harmony of life. They must believe in themselves. They must trust in the spirits who brought them life.

Grandfather Fish spoke of the times when the fish were considered the most powerful of all creatures. Fish brought life to the rivers and streams. Those who fished for food never starved. Then all respect was lost when the men came and fished, only to brag and leave the fish spirits rotting on land. Grandfather Fish puckered his long lips, speaking harshly: "We still have our power. We still have the ability to control men by staying away from them and not being caught. The strength that we give them from our flesh shall be taken from them. We shall leave and stay away from them."

Oldest snake slithered, slowly circling the others. "We can still enter men's dreams," he said. "Men will dream of snakes wrapping around them in slimy folds and coming in and out of their mouths and their faces. The taste of dead flesh or decaying fish in their mouths will make them lose their appetites, sicken them, and kill them." It was agreed: There would be no hope or help for those abusing the lives of fish and snakes.

The birds, insects, and smaller animals had their council, and the great Grubworm was the chief. They all decided to give their points of view to the most powerful Grubworm. Then they would vote on whether man should stay on the earth. Frog spoke, saying, "We must limit the number of people on earth, for they are taking over." Bird said, "Man has hurt my people in so many ways. Some he has burned are now black; some he has bruised are now blue; some he has let bleed are now red. Man has hurt birds too much." Each bird, each insect, each small animal had a complaint and proof to back up the charges. No man was present to defend himself.

The birds, insects, and smaller animals and reptiles gathered in groups and devised plans to give man diseases. They thought up so many diseases that no man would live under this plan. Finally, they came to the conclusion that man was born of woman. If women were the ones affected by disease, fewer men would exist. The final decision came: When the women menstruated, they would die and so would human beings.

The Grubworm was so excited about this decision that he stood up and shook with joy. He shook and shook and shook and shook, then fell over backward and has been on his back ever since. He could not stand up to get a final vote.

The plants listened to the animals' complaints. The plants felt the destruction in the anger of these animals. The plants were friendly to man, who had watered them, nurtured them, and helped them grow. The plants decided to help man. The trees, shrubs, grasses, bushes, and herbs agreed to have a cure for each one of the diseases thought of by the animals. These cures were taught to people by the spirits, and slowly human beings learned to use the cures and to be more polite and thoughtful to other forms of life.

CHEROKEE PLANT MEDICINE

The Cherokee were agricultural people, their old ways filled with flora of the valleys and ridges of Tennessee, Georgia, and the Carolinas. Plants hold an important place in the mythology and ceremonies of this tribe, and many of the people's beliefs relate to the practice of medicine. The plants protect people and help them gain more power to live and protect others.

It is said that trees even gave warriors special powers in battle. Some men could rise to the tops of trees, showering arrows down on the enemy. If struck by an arrow, they would call the power of the tree into their being, and the wound would heal as if it had never been. Once the Shawano people and the Cherokee battled. The Cherokee leader stood tall, directly in front of the enemy. He let the whole of the Shawano party shoot at him, and he was not hurt. But then, the Shawano leader, who held the knowledge of medicine magic, ordered his men to shoot at the trees over the Cherokee leader's head. The Cherokee leader fell dead, for his power and strength came from the trees around him.

The Indian people were close observers of plants, and their naming proves it. One example is the mistletoe, which cannot survive alone; it is a parasite to cedar and other trees from which it gains its sustenance. The Cherokee call it **Uda'li,** *which means "the married one." Some plants received ceremonial names, such as* **atsil'sun'ti,** *which means "fire maker" because its dried stalk was used in producing fire by friction.* **Aniwani'ski,** *or "talkers" (bugleweed), was so named because the chewed root, given to children to swallow or rubbed on their lips, brought them the gift of speech. Ginseng was known as* **A'tali'guli,** *"the mountain climber," for it gave energy to those who needed it—even enough energy to climb the tallest mountain. Corn was referred to as* **selu',** *or "Old Woman."*

The separation of evergreens and deciduous trees comes to us through myth. The deciduous trees received punishment and were not allowed to be green all throughout the winter. The Yuchi, who were neighbors of the Cherokee, relate the story.

2. Cedar Tree Medicine

The Yuchi myth tells of an evil medicine man who stopped the course of the sun every day. The pleasure that he received from this action was questionable. He brought obvious problems upon the people. Stopping the sun in the middle of the day threw off the planting, birthing, and healing of the people. The people asked him to stop this practice, but he only smiled. Sun grew tired of waiting for this medicine man to release him and burned hotter and hotter. This made matters worse. Healers called on the spirits for wisdom. Mothers kept their children inside for fear of their burning or of being taken by this evil medicine man for other testings. It was not a good time. The evil medicine man felt power in this controversy, and the people felt helpless.

Two strong warriors were asked to come forward and kill this evil one. This was not easy, for the evil power that this medicine man held went past life as they knew it, past reason as they knew it, and beyond the spirit world as they knew it. The warriors were trained, taught, and put through incredible testings to carry out this plan.

The two warriors finally achieved their power strength. They caught up this evil medicine man and cut his head off. They cut it off as they chanted and pulled the power of the good spirits to them. Evil spirits flew through the air and around the bodies of the two warriors. They whirled around the head as the warriors separated it from the body of the dead medicine man. The head came off but did not die. It spoke, and the words were more horrid and evil than before.

Frightened warriors pushed away their fear to pull in the power of knowledge. They took the head and tied it to a tree. It continued to speak. The fear that they held away from them started to move closer. They would not let it enter their thoughts;

they had to protect their people. They removed the head and tied it to the top of another tree. They tied it as high as they could so as not to hear the foul words that fell from the severed head's lips. Still it continued to speak.

In the morning, when they went to check on the severed head, they found it at the base of the tree still spouting horrible, evil words. They continued to tie it to the tops of trees, hoping to find the right tree that would quiet the head's evil ways. Trees were the spirit holders of good, and they held the magic of healing. Tree bark, tree leaves, needles, and nuts had saved many of the people's lives, and these warriors put their trust in the trees.

One night, after they had tied the severed head to the top of an ancient cedar tree, they hurried back to their camp. The scruffy cedar had jabbed them with needles, and its rough bark had torn their skin. The warriors were busy applying salve and grease to their wounds. This had been a difficult tree, with its bent branches and hard, bony knots. They would not want to climb this tree again.

The words of the evil severed head carried in the wind. The words entered the warriors' heads as they dreamed. At dawn, when the sun reached over the earth to awaken them, they continued to sleep. The sharp, evil words were now quiet. These two warriors slept peacefully until the birds of morning sang them awake.

They were startled at the length of time they had remained asleep. They listened to the quiet. The wind was soft; their thoughts were their own; their spirits no longer were threatened with evil words of fear.

They ran to the old scruffy cedar tree, where the severed head was dripping blood down the tree's bark. The head had finally died. The evil head could not find a way down the bent branches and hard, bony knots. Cedar needles stuck out of its eye sockets and mouth. The cedar tree had held the evil head, drawing the evil blood that dripped down the bark. That is why the cedar has blood-red bark and is known as a medicine tree that fights evil and sickness.

SACRED TREES

The Omaha, Ponka, Kansa, and Osage of the Sioux group have two sacred trees, the ash and the cedar. The ash is connected with the most powerful of healing medicine. Part of the sacred pole used by the Omaha and the Ponka was made of the ash, as were the stems of the sacred pipes, called **niniba weawa.**

For many people, cedar is associated with powerful forces and mystery. The Santee Dakota use it in their ceremony of the four winds. The Teton Dakota believe that the smell of cedar wood has curing properties and that cedar smoke keeps away ghosts. The Hidatsa people believe that the red cedar tree is both mysterious and sacred.

In short, the power of trees can bring about healings and visions, which themselves work in several ways. Some visions take the form of animals talking to people. The animals give power by allowing human beings to assume their forms or to understand their language; or they may give other sorts of gifts. The animals also can save people from danger and bring them success in life.

The second power from visions comes with the appearance of clouds (or human shapes having wings like eagles) and human voices. These visions allow people to foretell the future and to know the character of anyone they meet.

The third power from visions relates only to the hearing of voices. There is no apparition and no change of shape. The voices give hearers the power to achieve success and to foresee oncoming death.

Visions were known by all people, and such visions were real. They affected one's life forever and held a power rarely explainable.

3. Hozin'i Chant

The Navaho tell of a healing—a *beauty* healing, for lack of a better English word. This healing was learned through a great adventure.

Once, Turtle, Frog, Snake, and Bear ventured out in search of women. They walked for some time until they came to a river. At the stream Bear listened. The river told him that only Snake and Bear should go ahead. Turtle and Frog were to wait, and Wind would tell them when to help Bear and Snake.

Bear and Snake walked along the river until they came to a place where there was dancing. Bear and Snake changed shape. Bear changed into a fine young man with a bear-claw necklace around his neck. Snake changed into a fine young man with snake skins braided into his hair.

They walked to the dance. At the dance were two women. One had white shells wrapped into her hair whorls. The other had turquoise strung into her hair. The women were beautiful. Snake asked the one with turquoise if she would come with him after the dance. She said, "No."

Bear asked the one with the white shells if she would come with him after the dance. She said, "No."

Bear was disappointed, so he and Snake talked and decided on a way to trick the women. They waded across the river and built a lodge. There they sat outside and smoked a unique tobacco. It smelled very good.

The women smelled the tobacco. The woman with the white shells waded across the river to Bear. The woman with the turquoise waded across the river to Snake. They asked if they could have some smoke. Bear shook his head. "It would not be right," he said, "for women that we do not know to be seen smoking with us away from the dance."

The woman with the white shells smiled at the two men. "We could go into your lodge and smoke with you. No one would see us there."

The four of them went into the lodge. There they smoked. It was a sacred smoke, and they fell asleep. When the women awoke, they were held by Bear and Snake. Snake had turned back into a snake and had wrapped his body around the woman with turquoise in her hair. Bear had put his bear-claw necklace around the woman with the white shells in her hair. The necklace held her to him. The women were frightened. They spoke softly while Bear and Snake slept.

"We must leave here," they said. "How can we get away?" Every time the woman with the turquoise in her hair moved, Snake grabbed her tightly. This woman's name was Glipspa. The other woman with the shell in her hair also tried to move, but Bear reached up and knocked her head off. Glipspa was terrified. She knew that she had to get away. She relaxed and quietly slid out of Snake's grasp. She escaped from the lodge and ran for her home.

Bear awoke and saw the woman's head on the floor of the lodge. He woke up Snake and said, "Come, we must go." Snake drew his knife, removing the scalp of the beheaded woman with the shells in her hair. Bear and Snake walked hurriedly to the river and started back to Turtle and Frog. They met Turtle and Frog, and gave them the scalp with the shells.

Glipspa hurried on. As she came around the corner to her home, she saw her father talking with some other men. Her father was saying, "If I find that daughter of mine, I will kill her and hang her body on a pole in the center of the village to show the others." The rest of the men nodded in agreement. The father said, "Let us search for her and give her the punishment she deserves."

Glipspa ran out of the village and raced for the flat desert land. She ran and ran until she found a place to hide. She scrounged for some food and fell sound asleep. The sacred smoke from the night before still made her tired and sad.

Frog and Turtle took the scalp and started back to their village. Snake and Bear followed them for awhile. Soon, they came across some young hunters. The group of young men decided to have a contest to see who could shoot the best and set up a target. They each took turns shooting. The others would laugh or nod depending on the hit of the arrow. Snake and Bear came forward and asked if they could shoot. The young men smiled and nodded. They thought that these old ones would never strike the target.

Snake shot his arrow and hit the target. The young men were impressed and nodded, mumbling to each other. Bear pulled a long, sharp arrow from his quiver, retracted his claws, and shot, splitting the arrow that Snake had shot. The young men nodded, their eyes wide. Turtle came forward and shot at the target, knocking off the split arrow. Then Frog came forward. As he pulled the bow from his side, the scalp he had tied to his belt fell on the ground.

The group of young men saw this scalp. They knew who it belonged to, and they watched Frog shoot. Snake and Bear saw what had happened as well, and they disappeared up the river road. Turtle waited as Frog shot and split his arrow at the target. Turtle became angry and was ready to strike Frog's arrow, when the young men took both prisoner.

They tied them up and carried them to their village. The people were sad when they saw the scalp. They took Frog and Turtle and placed them inside a great cooking pot. The people built a huge fire. They started to boil Frog and Turtle; but Frog was filled with water, and as the cooking pot became hot, he leaned over and spewed water on the fire. The fire was put out, and the people were angry.

They took Frog and Turtle, tied them to a tree, and shot arrows at the two. Frog stood behind Turtle, and his shell was so hard that the arrows bounced off. This made the people even angrier. They took Frog and Turtle and threw them into the river to drown them. But Frog and Turtle swam away, down to the place where Snake and Bear were waiting for them. Then they went home.

Glipspa awoke at the edge of the desert. She was very thirsty and knew that she would have to find water somewhere. She ran into the desert, searching for a water cache. There was none. She looked up on the horizon and saw a large lake. She ran to the lake, but when she put her hand down to lift the water to her mouth, the lake was hard. She could not get her hand into the water. It was hard as a rock.

Glipspa stood there and let her tears strike the water. They splashed on the hard water and were not absorbed. She was puzzled, scared, and still thirsty. She looked toward the sky and said a prayer. As she spoke, the lake lifted up off the ground. When she looked down, she saw a village under this lake of hard water. She walked down into the village.

There in the village were people. They greeted her and motioned for her to come eat and drink. She did so. They invited her to stay with them. She did so. She was adopted into a family and there met a fine young man. She stayed with him and worked. Each night, she would walk and think of her home.

One night as she walked, she came across the man she had chosen. He was speaking with some others, and they did not notice her. They all turned into snakes and began to slither around in a circle. They had many colors of corn meal in this circle. As they slithered, they made a beautiful design in the sand. She was amazed at this and walked closer. They saw her.

Her man did not turn back into a person; he remained a snake and slithered after her. His sharp tongue darted back and forth, and his fangs sparkled in the moonlight. She was terrified. She ran, and ran, and ran, and ran from there. She ran to the edge of the lake and said a prayer. The lake lifted up into the air, and she ran.

Her man turned into a person. He followed her and finally caught her. He carried her back to their home. He set her down, told her that the sacred corn meal pattern they were making was called the *Hozin'i*, and instructed her to learn this ceremony since she had witnessed it.

Her man taught her all—the chant, how to grind the corn, how to place the colors, how to heal the people with the chant.

Glipspa learned quickly and felt the power of this ceremony. She remained with these people.

One morning, she awoke and was very ill. She could not eat nor move, and her skin was dry and hurt. She was not well. Her man felt sorry for her. He tried to heal her. He rubbed grease on her skin, but it remained dry. He gave her teas, but her stomach would not accept food. Her man held her in his arms and sang to her, but her eyes glazed over, and she did not appear to heal.

The elder of the group was asked to come and see Glipspa. He spoke with her and then spoke with her man. "It is time," he said, "for this one to go home and teach her people of this ceremony. It is selfish for us to keep her here. She must share this ceremony with those of her way. She will do this. She will come back. You must trust in your union and trust in your woman. She is strong and she will come back."

Glipspa and her man walked out from under the lake. Her man accompanied her. He stopped outside the village and told her, "You are here to do what you must do. I am doing this as I must do. You are part of me. I will never be without you in my spirit. My spirit goes with you." Glipspa studied her man's eyes. She saw herself in his eyes. She believed him.

Glipspa walked to her home. Her mother and father were happy to see her. They had aged greatly. Her brother was now a man of great respect, and he also had aged. Glipspa took her brother aside. She told him of the ceremony and tried to teach him of it.

She helped him grow the corn that she had brought with her. She showed him how to grind the corn and use the pollen. She taught him the chants and the songs. Yet he would not learn. He could follow her, but when left alone he could not remember. Glipspa fell asleep with a troubled mind. Her brother was not learning. She dreamed of her man; she dreamed of him making teas; she dreamed of him showing her how to sing and work with her brother.

Next morning, she met her brother as he was gathering more corn. She took her brother aside and made him teas with each of the different colors of corn. She made him drink each tea separately. She made him sing with her. She told him to lie down with his head in her lap. She stroked his hair back, and she sang to him over, and over, and over, and over. She did this for four days.

On the fifth morning, her brother sat up and rubbed his eyes. "I know it now," he said. "I shall show you that now I can do this." He took the corn meal and drew the right picture. He sang the right songs. He chanted the right chant. He did as he was taught by his sister without any help at all.

Glipspa taught him the ways of healing and helping others to feel beautiful and good within themselves. Glipspa watched as her brother then continued to teach others. When they would not learn, she showed him how to make the teas, sing the songs, and perform the dream rituals. It was good. It worked.

Glipspa packed up her things. She said good-bye to her old mother and old father. She smiled on her brother, who was now wise in the ways of the *Hozin'i* chant. She walked into the desert and searched and searched for the lake. She could not find it. She sat down and unrolled her cloth bundle of corn meal. She took each color and laid it out on the ground. There in front of her appeared her man.

He rubbed out the corn meal with his foot. He lifted her off the ground with his strength, placed her beside him, and smiled, saying, "You have come back. You have come back. I dreamed of you asking me for wisdom. I knew you would return."

They went together to the village under the lake, and it is known that she is still there. This is the way of the *Hozin'i* chant.

4. Kiowa Medicine House

The Kiowa traditionally had a medicine house, usually situated near the center of an encampment. It was circular and about sixty feet in diameter, with the entrance facing east. For support, the house had a central, forked post, twenty feet high. Around it were placed seventeen other posts, forming the outline of the building. These posts were from twelve to fifteen feet high and made of cottonwood, and to them—with their limbs and leaves—whole cottonwood trees were tied horizontally by ropes of rawhide. Outside these small cottonwood trees was placed a wall of green trees several feet thick, and in the midst of this were many hundreds of spectators, who in the cool shade could observe what was going on without making themselves conspicuous.

The central post was ornamented near the ground with the robes of buffalo calves with their heads upward, as if they were trying to climb the poles. Each one of the branches above the forks was ornamented in a similar manner with the strips of colorful shawls, calico cloth, scarves...and these were covered at the top with black muslin.

The spiritual ceremony of the Kiowa was the *K'ad'o*, or sun dance, celebrated in the middle of June. Their calendar system was counted by *K'ad'os*, the winters being designated as "cold seasons." The whole tribe would camp in a circle, each band in its traditional location, with the *K'ad'o*, or medicine lodge, in the center. Within the medicine lodge was the sacred spear of the *taime*.

The Kiowa sun dance resembled that of the Dakota, Cheyenne, and other tribes in its general features—the great search for the buffalo; the camp circle; the procession of the women to cut down the tree for the center pole of the sacred medicine lodge; and the battle for the possession of the pole; the building of the medicine lodge; and the four days of dancing without eating, drinking, or sleeping.

The medicine lodge was a place of healing, testing, perfect faith; and the people's most sacred objects were the *A'dalbeahya,* the *taime,* the *Gadombitsonhi,* and the *seni,* or peyote. Their tribal religion itself centered on the *A'dalbeahya* and the *taime.*

The *A'dalbeahya* (*adal* = hair or scalp) was the eucharistic body of their Great Spirit, Hero-Teacher Sun-Boy, known to the people from the beginning of all time. Sun-Boy was the son of a young girl who was playing one day with some companions when she discovered a porcupine in the branches of a tree. She climbed up to capture it. As she climbed, the tree grew taller, and taller, and taller, and taller, carrying her with it.

The tree pierced the arch of the sky into the upper world. Here, the porcupine took on his proper form as the Son of the Sun. They were married and she bore a son. Her husband warned her that if she were to search for food, berries, roots, and nuts, she must never go near the plant called the *azon* (pomme blanche), for the top of it had been bitten off by a buffalo.

She dreamed of the *azon* and her craving grew. Finally, she could not resist, and she dug up the plant, pulling it up by the root and leaving a hole through which she saw, far below, the earth that she had left behind the day she climbed the tree. She ached to return.

She took her child and, fastening a rope above the hole, let herself and the child down to the earth. Her husband discovered her missing, and his anger grew at her betrayal. He took a rock and struck her upon the head. She fell dead to the ground, but her child continued down, tied to the rope, and landed uninjured. After staying some time by his mother's body, he was found and cared for by Spider Woman. She became his second mother.

One day he was playing with a gaming wheel, throwing it up into the air and catching it. This time, when he threw it up into the air, it came down with the bright sun in his eyes. It fell and landed upon his head, cutting through his body and making twin brothers out of the one. After many testings, the twins walked into the waters upon the earth and left behind a sacred "medicine" in ten portions. This came to be called *A'dalbeahya*, and it was kept by the priests and healers.

The *Gadombitsonky*, "Old-Woman-Under-the-Ground," belonged to the Kinep band of the healers of the Kiowa. She was a tiny woman, less than a foot high, with flowing hair. Once she was exposed in front of the *taime* at the great sun-dance ceremony, and by some unexplained magic, the priest in charge caused her to rise out of the ground, dance with the people, and then sink down again. A crazy Indian healer gathered her up and guarded her, and she was never seen again after this.

The *seni* is the prickly fruit of the peyote or mescal plant, a small species of cactus of the genus *Lophophora* that grows in the stony hills along the Mexican border. It has a great healing effect and, when used in ceremony, causes myths and rituals to come to life.

The most sacred and greatest central figure of the sun-dance ceremony was the *taime.* This was a small image, less than two feet high, representing a human figure dressed in a robe of white feathers, with a headdress of one upright feather. It had pendants of ermine skin with numerous strands of blue beads around the neck. The face, breast, and back were painted with designs of the sun and the moon.

The figure itself was of dark-green stone, roughly resembling a human head and shaped like the fetishes of the Pueblo tribes. Preserved in a rawhide box watched over by a sacred healer, it was never seen except at the annual sun dance, when it was fastened to a short, upright stick planted within the medicine lodge near the western side.

The ancient *taime* (predecessor of this stone) was of buckskin, with a stalk of Indian tobacco for a headdress. Actually, there was more than one *taime* involving more than one tribe. Its myth was told in the oral manner:

There was a poor Arapaho who had no horse. He had no food. He had no honor. He went to the Crow people and asked to participate in the ceremony. He danced long before the ceremony started and with great sincerity. He danced long after the ceremony in prayer that the ceremony would make him a wealthy man. The chief of the priests of the Crow people then gave him the *taime.*

The Crow were quite angry with the priest, for he was showing favoritism to the stranger. Fortune came to the poor Arapaho. He gained in strength and courage. He stole horses through raids and battles. He soon held the largest number of horses in the area. He returned to the Crow people and gave thanks to the priest for the strength of the ceremony. As he collected his horses to leave, the Crow followed.

At night they crept into his camp and stole back the *taime* bag from the pole in front of his tipi. When he discovered the loss of the *taime,* the Arapaho made his own and carried the bags with him, shared them with his people, and became powerful with the giving of them. Later, he married a Kiowa woman and went to live with her tribe. He took his *taime* bags with him, and this became the medicine of the Kiowa. Since that time the *taime* has been passed from generation to generation, and the keeper of the *taime* bags has always been of part-Arapaho blood line. The medicine way was now moved from one group of people to another.

5. Buffalo-Dung Boy

The Blackfeet were plagued with monsters. Monsters everywhere ate the children, attacked them in the night, and stole what they had worked so hard to hunt. It was a miserable time for the Blackfeet. They chanted and prayed, hoping that someone would come and save them from total destruction.

Traveling with them, at this time, were an elderly man and his woman. They had no family, only each other. If one of them were to die, the other would follow soon after, and this made them sad. They walked along behind the others, and their age made them noticeably different, as well as slow. The other Blackfeet moved way in front of them as they talked and tried to keep pace.

This man and woman had a strong love for each other, but their union had not brought them children. The people believed that if a man and woman were pure of heart and strong in spirit, children would be a gift to them from the spirits. These two were pure in heart. They were strong in spirit and worked hard for the people, yet they did not have children. An elder told them that once life was given to a man and woman, they must know how to care for that life. If they did not raise that child to learn of harmony, the child would be taken from them. The couple knew of this. They were appreciative and knowledgeable of life, and willing to learn of the pleasures of raising children. These two people were ready for life to come to them. They thought they knew.

Sun heard these two talking about children again. Sun felt their age and knew of their hearts. Sun let the heat from his strength warm the earth and soften her feelings. Earth let the old ones walk across the sloping breast of her hills. Earth heard them talking again of wanting children. Earth knew of their goodness and their strength. Earth let the warmth of Sun radiate from her being to the old ones.

The elderly man and the elderly woman became tired. Their people were far ahead of them. The elderly man took two of the poles from the wrapped bundle he dragged behind him and built a simple structure. He helped his woman as she lay down next to him in the shade. Their hands were held in firm embrace as they fell asleep. The elderly man learned in a dream that if they each cut their bodies and placed a small amount of blood together, the sun would dry it to be one clot of blood. The two of them were to have their union in such a way.

The woman dreamed that she was to place their clot of blood into a buffalo-dung chip. The blood clot was then to be removed and placed in a bowl with the buffalo-dung chip on top of it and water added. They were to cook this pot of blood and dung over a small fire outside. A child would be born in the pot if they followed this dream.

The elderly woman awoke first. She walked to a piece of buffalo dung and sighed. "This piece of buffalo dung has no blood in it," she said.

Her elderly man came over, gently lifted her robe, and cut her flesh until it bled. She did not stop him, for she believed in him. He cut his flesh until it bled. The sun shone down on them as the two drops of blood formed one blood clot on the buffalo-dung chip.

The elderly man reached down and picked it up, cradling it in his arms. "We shall have life," he said. "We shall have life as strong as the buffalo."

Yet his woman was concerned. "We have no fire," she said, "with which to continue."

The man studied her face. The lines of time had been kind to her. She still held great beauty. "We shall walk, and the wood will be there," he said. "We must believe in what we feel, in what we know, in what the spirits have told us. Come."

The elderly man lifted up their belongings. The elderly woman cradled the buffalo-dung chip. They moved until the sun was ready to go to the place of night. Sun shone with a red-yellow hue.

The elderly man put down his belongings. He put the buffalo dung down as he helped his woman sit on the ground. He helped her become comfortable, and then he placed the buffalo dung in her lap. "Stay here," he said. "I shall return."

He walked away from her, searching for firewood. There was not much where they were, but he found enough to make a fire. He built the fire using the wood sparingly. His elderly woman rocked the buffalo dung, thinking of the life that could come from her body and trying to give this piece of buffalo dung part of her spirit.

Her elderly man washed his body with sacred pollen. He chanted into the fire. He did as his woman told him. He took the buffalo dung from his woman and removed the blood clot from the dung. He dropped the blood clot into a bowl of boiling water and put the dung over it. He took his woman and washed her in sacred corn pollen from his medicine pouch. They chanted together and became tired, soon falling asleep.

They both dreamed of a baby and how he would help them and the Blackfeet people. They awoke to the sound of a baby crying. There in the pot was a small baby boy. They quickly removed him, and the elderly woman held him to her breast. Milk flowed freely from her into the baby's mouth.

On the fourth day, the baby boy spoke. He said, "Tie me to four poles that need to be placed here."

The elderly man walked for four days and returned with four poles. He set them up as had been requested. Next, the baby told his adopted father, "Tie me now to these poles; then take a birch rod and lash me with it." The elderly man was hesitant, but he did as he was asked. The baby boy grew with each lashing and soon was a strong man.

The strong man grew not only in body, but in spirit power and strength. He carried his adopted mother and father to the Blackfeet people. He became known as the Buffalo-Dung Boy. He fought the monsters and became known as *Kut-o-yis.* He saved the Blackfeet people and took care of his adopted parents.

6. Ani-kuta-ni

The Cherokee were at one time a large group of people who had many different traditions and tribal names. One of these was the *Ani-kuta-ni,* also known as the *Ani-kwata-ni.* They were considered an ancient people who preceded the Cherokee and built mounds, though some believe that the Ani-kuta-ni were destroyed long before the Cherokee became a people.

The old ones of the Cherokee people tell of the *Ani-kuta-ni* as those who held the magic and understanding of the earth and all life around them. A grandfather spoke of the ability of the Cherokee *Ani-kuta-ni* medicine man who knew if a person would heal or not before even attempting a medical cure. Tradition held that if a person living among these people was considered of higher spirit value than another, there was no point in attempting a cure, for the spirit would heal the sickness. But if someone did not have the spirit quality that could help him or her, the medicine man would come in and provide a cure.

It is told by the old ones that the *Ani-kuta-ni* were massacred by others holding similar powers. These people were known as the *Nai'kuta-ni.* They were a mystical religious body with unbelievable powers. They once stole the beautiful wife of an *Ani-kuta-ni* chief. So the *Ani-kuta-ni* chief and his people slaughtered a great number of the *Nai'kuta-ni;* and the *Nai'kuta-ni,* in turn, killed many of them. This was considered a contributing factor to the perishing of the hereditary secret society. Since that time, the old ones say there have been no hereditary privileges tolerated among the Cherokees.

The *Ani-kuta-ni* had medicine to alter their forms as they pleased: they were known as shape-changers. Once, one of the medicine warriors came home from an expedition and found that his people were under attack by a large group. Most of the men who were the strongest warriors of the *Ani-kuta-ni* were away hunting. This warrior made up his mind that he would save his grandmother from the battle.

This warrior set off from his village. He walked along the river and found a mussel shell. He took his medicine pouch and changed the mussel shell into a canoe. He crossed the river to his grandmother's house. She was seated there, waiting for the enemy to come and kill her, for she had given up all hope of being saved. This warrior took his medicine pouch and put his grandmother into a small gourd, which he fastened to his belt. The warrior climbed a tree and changed himself into a swamp woodcock, and with one loud cry, he spread his wings and flew across to the other side of the river. Safely landing there, he changed both of them back to their normal shapes, and they made their way through the woods to another village.

7. Uktena

Long ago the old ones tell of *Hilahi'yu* when the earth was just here. Sun became angry at the disrespectful people on earth and sent a horrible sickness to destroy them. Little Men of the earth [people] changed a man into a Monster Snake, which they called *Uktena,* also known as the spirit "Keen-eyed." *Uktena* was sent to kill Sun. *Uktena* failed.

Then Little Men sent Rattlesnake Spirit to kill Sun. *Uktena* became jealous and vicious to the Little Men. Little Men grew afraid and took their powers, sending *Uktena* up to *Galun'lati,* the place of the dangerous things. *Uktena* left others behind that were as dangerous as he was. He had them hide in deep pools in the river or in the lonely passes of the high mountains. These became known as the "snake spirits that keep people."

Those who know of *Uktena* know him as a great snake, wide as a tree trunk, with horns on his head and a bright, blazing crest like a shining diamond on his forehead. His scales glitter like sparks of fire. He has rings and spots of color along his whole length and cannot be wounded except by shooting in the seventh spot from the head, because it is here that his heart and life spirit hide. The shining diamond is referred to as the *Ulunsu'ti,* and whoever owns this is sure to have success in hunting, healing, growing, and in every part of human business. Healers use it in their work.

Uktena came to the people with the help of two brothers. They were hunting together, and when they came to a camping place in the mountains, they made a fire. One gathered wood to put up a shelter, and the other went up the creek to look for a deer. The one who was hunting heard a noise—like two animals fighting—on the top of the ridge. He hurried to see what it might be, and there he found the great *Uktena* coiled around a man.

Uktena was choking the man. The man was fighting for his life and called out to the hunter, "Help me. He is your enemy as well as mine!" The hunter took aim, drew back his arrow to the head of *Uktena,* and shot. It went through the body, and blood spouted from the hole. The snake loosed its coils with a snapping noise and went tumbling down the ridge, tearing up the earth as he fell.

The stranger stood up, and it was the great *Asga'ya Gi'gaei,* the Red Man of Lightning. He said to the hunter, "You have helped me, and now I will reward you. I shall give you a medicine that will help you always find game."

They waited until the day was night and then went down the ridge where the dead *Uktena* had rolled. The birds and insects· had now eaten the body, and all that was left were the bones. In one place were flashes of light coming up from the ground. Flashes of light moved in the darkness. Red Man of Lightning took the light and showed it to the hunter. It was a scale of *Uktena.* Red Man of Lightning went over to a tree that had been struck by lightning and gathered splinters. Then he made a fire and burned *Uktena's* scale to a coal. He wrapped this in a piece of deerskin and gave it to the hunter, saying, "As long as you have this, you will always find game to hunt and food for your family. You shall never know hunger."

Red Man of Lightning told the hunter to go back to camp and hang up the medicine on a tree outside, because it was very strong and dangerous. He told him he would find his brother nearly dead in the cabin. This would be caused from the power of *Uktena's* scale. The hunter then must take a small piece of cane, which the Red Man of Lightning gave him, scrape a little of it into water, and give it to his brother to drink. This would make his brother well again.

Then the Red Man of Lightning disappeared. The hunter could not see where he went. He returned to his camp and found his brother gasping for life. The hunter did as he was taught, and his brother was cured with the cane water. This healing was never forgotten, and the power of *Uktena's* scale and cane became part of the Cherokee way.

8. Dasi-giya-gi

Dasi-giya-gi was a famous Cherokee warrior. His friends knew him as Shoe-boots, and he once lived on Hightower Creek in Georgia. He could change shape and take on the power of many. Some saw him throw a corn *matate,* or mortar, over a house. He was known for leaping wide rivers that were deep and dangerous. It was said that his medicine power was from *Uktena's* scale and a large turtle shell that he traded from the Shawano people.

Shoe-boots fought in the Creek War using his medicine magic. He put *Uktena's* scale into the water and bathed his body. He took the turtle shell and drew a black line around his men with coal: he never was wounded, and none of his men were killed. Shoe-boots brought back the belief in medicine, which aided many. Some warriors could dive under the ground as if it were water, come up in the center of an enemy camp to kill and scalp their foes, and then dive back down under the ground, returning to their own camp.

9. Delaware Hunter

The bear was the largest this one had ever seen. The size loomed over him as he tried to steady his bow and arrow. The breath of the bear fell down upon this hunter, pushing him to his knees. The bear's mouth was large, large enough for six deer to be eaten in one swallow. This hunter quivered as he tried to steady his hand. The bear bellowed, trees bent, clouds moved, and the hunter pulled, pulled, pulled, pulled from within him the strength of his father, his father's father, and his father's father's father, and his father's father's father's father. The strength filled him, reaching his shoulders, his arms, his hand, and his fingers.

The arrow flew, not to the bear's neck or heart, but straight to the bear's backbone. The sound of the crack echoed through the land. The hunter fell forward. He cupped his hands over his ears, and his heart stopped with the piercing, searing sound that came from this huge bear's throat. The bear fell but five feet from him. The bear fell dead.

The hunter lifted his head and studied the bear. The bear's mouth was open, but there was no breath. The hunter crawled slowly over to the bear. The bear's chest heaved and was still.

The hunter stood over the bear and said, "Bear, you were no brave hunter. You instilled fear and terror, but you did not fight. Were you a brave hunter or warrior as you pretended to be, I would have had to shoot again and again. I would have come away scarred and bloody. But you did not fight."

The hunter pulled his sharp knife out of his belt and continued: "You have now found my people too powerful for you, yet if you had fought with me, I would have fought back with great courage, and I would have died as a brave warrior. Bear, I sit here and cry for you. You are a disgrace to your tribe, your people." The hunter knelt and sat back on his heels.

"Bear," he said, "you have lost your power to me, and I leave your weakness here for someone else to pick up and take with him."

The hunter cut the bear's neck and let the blood flow on the forest floor. Weakness was left behind to warn others, and the bear's meat was taken home to bring strength to all who ate it.

The bear, however, did not have bows and arrows with which to fight back.

Myths

Native Americans have a traditional ideology explaining the origin and nature of everything: their cosmology is the connective tissue to the world and life. Reality is divided into two planes or worlds, each holding power in healing. And healing itself does not end with curing individual ailments; it is a basic process of restoring balance to the universe.

Healing is needed not only for human beings, but also for animals. Illness or disharmony relates to misconceptions, spiritual loss, and the development of that which is wrong.

The power of the healing relates to the spirit plane being called upon to help with the cure. There is the mythical (which supernatural beings brought to make the world and give it its present shape and condition). Likewise, there is a world of ordinary, everyday existence.

The earth is physically as it is; yet to live on it and understand its powers, one must understand the four horizontal layers. The lowest one in the Pueblo region is yellow; the one above, blue-green; the third, red; and the top layer is known as the White-

House World. Healers call upon this division of colors, upon certain directions, and upon special plants and animals. Each direction, or cardinal point, holds spiritual cures, and each is traditionally associated with a color, a mountain, a warrior, a woman with an appropriately colored face, an animal, a bird, a snake, or a tree. All of this information must be known to restore harmony, balance, integrity, health.

The relationship of each spirit to the other is important in traditional healing. No part of life can be separated from another. Each story, each spirit, each birth of each spirit, each spiritual power holder has the value of life itself. To be wise in the ways of healing, one must value each spirit and understand which spirit is needed. Therefore, this chapter deals with the birth of each spirit—the story of creation as it exists within the culture that values it. All this is relevant to the culture's language, values, traditions, and, ultimately, to its surviving disease.

All of life is intertwined and cannot be pulled apart at a whim. Healing takes all that is from the beginning of time to the present, as well as the hopes of the future, and uses all of it to call for spirits' help in the healing.

The concept of healing was at one time linked to cultist beliefs. Healings included a system of beliefs, with elaborate systems of rites, and ceremonies directly connecting medicine and philosophy.

The stories that follow relate to the religious beliefs as they began with creation. The basis of healing flows from the beliefs of the People, the term used here for Native Americans. The natural is small and quiet and mysterious, while the mystic supernatural is large and overspreads most of the healing experience and thought. Thus, animals, plants, and even inorganic objects are filled with mysterious qualities and powers that come from their association with the unusual or unexpected.

It is difficult to divide phenomena, as they appear to the Native-American mind, into the human and superhuman experience, for they are one. Man himself may become a spirit or a healing-spirit by fasting, prayer, and vision. To become a spirit, one must know the ways of the spirits and where these spirits came from. Once this is grasped, the knowledge of the healing will follow.

*The most sacred beliefs reach back to the beginning, and they hold the power of all life. Many of these stories were traditionally concealed from strangers to protect the most sacred ways of life. They are shared now with the understanding that through belief or religion comes the warming of the heart. Healing through ceremony is brought about from the knowledge of **creation**, which is the finest gift of all.*

1. Male Healing

Before the beginning, Awanawilona was the All Father. There was nothing else in the black darkness except Awanawilona. The time of the New-Made had come.

Awanawilona conceived life. Awanawilona became Sun Father, the All Father, the conceiver of what was and is. His appearance made bright the place of cloud mist. The cloud mist gathered with the brightness and rained down to become the Place of the Water Holding.

Sun Father took his *Yepnane*, his essence, and germinated the Place of the Water Holding. This combination of the heat and light, the moistness of the water, and *Yepnane* essence formed green foam that rose up on the water and became Awitellin Tsita, the Four Point Holder of Life Earth Mother. Awitellin Tsita grew round and large with the life that grew within her. From this came a separation known as Apoyan Ta'chu, the All-Covering Father Sky.

The germinated substance of life grew, spewing out the grasses, trees, and flowers. Deep down inside Awitellin Tsita, life stirred and grew. She became massive and dense with growing heaviness.

Father Sky found her too big to hold. He let her fall down into the Place of the Water Holding, leaving only portions of her in sight of Sun Father.

Earth Mother Awitellin Tsita felt her form changing; felt a fear of the unborn; felt unsure of her ability to care for what would be. She called up to Sun Father Apoyan Ta'chu, "How will the life that we have made find its way up to the bright light of your wisdom? How will the new ones know of the path?"

Sun Father Apoyan Ta'chu changed his shape and took the form of man. Sun Father Apoyan Ta'chu blew smoke upon Earth

Mother Awitellin Tsita, and she took the form of woman. She lifted mud from the waters around her feet and made a clay bowl.

"This," she said, "is the land my children will have. They will wander along the edge of the bowl, searching for food and drinking the water."

She spat into the bowl and stirred the foam with her finger. "The nourishment from my bosom shall feed them," she said, "and they will grow. The moisture from your body, Father Sky Apoyan Ta'chu, will feed the earth and make food for all in this place."

Father Sky Apoyan Ta'chu nodded and said, "White clouds shall float up from the water at the edges of your earth. And the clusters of mud shall be the mountains, and the mountains shall have terraced gardens for food, and the soul-beings shall feed off these, which will be watered from the essence of my being. The offspring shall eat and grow, and I shall cover them with the rain-spray of my being to bring warmth and coldness, water and nurturing."

Sky Father Apoyan Ta'chu rubbed his hands together, and when he opened them, there were gleaming sparks of coal that turned golden.

"These," he announced, "shall feed the children."

Then he took the golden grains and dropped them into the bowl held in Earth Mother's hand. "These golden-grain seeds shall grow and feed the children," he said. "Seed grains touched by my water essence shall spring up from your bosom."

Tall, golden ears of corn developed from the long green stalks rising up from the bowl.

The fourth deepest womb of Mother Earth Woman held the seeds of mankind and the creatures of all. They each took form and multiplied. This fourth deepest womb was known as Anosin Tehuli because it was dark, black as coal on a moonless night, and filled with a stench. The fourth and deepest womb, Anosin Tehuli, became filled until there was no more room for another creature in this place.

Poshaiyank'ya came out of this growth. Poshaiyank'ya appeared in the water, and with his wisdom he lifted up through the wombs to the bright world of Father Sky Apoyan Ta'chu.

Poshaiyank'ya called out to Father Sky Apoyan Ta'chu and told him of the crowding in Anosin Tehuli. Father Sky Apoyan Ta'chu studied Mother Earth Woman.

The Place of Water Holding had a large mass of foam floating aimlessly about it. Father Sky Apoyan Ta'chu directed a ray of his sunlight upon this foamy mass. The foam grew and ruptured at the side, giving birth to Unam Achi Piahkoa, the Healer of the Rain.

Then Unam Achi Piahkoa split apart, giving birth to the first Unam Ehkona (the Preceder, or Guide of Spiritual Matters) and Unam Yaluna (the Follower, or Overseer of Community Living). Out of the one came the two: the Preceder and the Follower, the Right and the Left, the Dark and the Light. They were as two brothers.

Father Sky Apoyan Ta'chu gave them wisdom from himself and wisdom from their mother. Father Sky Apoyan Ta'chu gave them the great Cloud-Bow and Arrows of Thunder of the four quarters. He gave them a Fog-Making shield that supported the wind, which circled the fog, keeping it close to the holder of the shield. Father Sky Apoyan Ta'chu also gave these two the right of fathership over all the creatures that were out of Father Sky Apoyan Ta'chu's sight and management. The two followed along the trail of Poshaiyank'ya to the fourth deepest womb. With their magic knives of the thunderbolt, they opened wide the paths and descended into the underworld.

The Preceder and the Follower took the tall grasses and long vines, braided them, and lifted the creatures up this green rope to the third womb.

All was good for a time.

The creatures multiplied and grew, and before long there was not enough room. This time the Preceder and the Follower grouped the people into bands. They had six kinds of men: the Yellow, the Tawny Grey, the Red, the White, the Mingled, and the Black.

They were led one on top of the other, hand-to-shoulder, hand-to-shoulder, up to the second womb. Here the light was brighter than in the other two wombs. The light entering was

enough to give wisdom to the people, creatures, and plants that were in this place of the second womb.

Many had fallen back down. Many were left behind, for they could not find the strength to move with the others.

This womb became crowded. This second womb was not large enough to hold all. The two brothers again lifted up the people, creatures, and plants to this place, Tek'ohaian-ulahnane, or the World of Knowledge.

People walked bent over from being in the low ceilings of this womb. Their eyes were covered with thin eyelids; their fingers and toes were webbed from being in the watery earth wombs; their skin was hard and scaly from protection in the dark. They had tails to give them balance. They were awkward.

The Bright Ones, stars, saw this and knew that the people would be blinded by the light of Father Sky Apoyan Ta'chu when he rose in the morning. So the Bright Ones thickened the people's eyelids, took away some of the people's webbing, removed the people's tails, and straightened the people's bodies. Father Sky Apoyan Ta'chu rose up to see his creations.

It was good. The creatures were strong; life moved forward. The Creation from the Male All Being now was Good, Strong, and As It Should Be.

2. Creation and Emergence

The creation of life brought about life. Male procreation brought life to fruition using the male strength of the sky. Male procreation could not be done alone. Tradition has it that there must be balance for survival. If life is out of balance, there will be illness, disease, and death of what we know now. Therefore, there must not only be male procreation but female procreation, or the male birth parallelling the female birth of life. Both are sacred, both are necessary, both are respected. Males are the germinators of life, and females are the reproducers of life; one cannot exist without the other.

Here, then, is the female creation and emergence of life:

The Overseer of this life became Tsityostinako
And her daughters, Uretsiti and Naot'siti.
There were clouds and fog in all four worlds.
They lived in the Yellow World for four years.
People multiplied and became many.
There were so many People that it was crowded.
There were too many in this place.
They asked if they could go to another place.
They asked Uretsiti and Naot'siti.
They asked the sisters.
The sisters asked Tsityostinako.
They asked their mother.
Tsityostinako said it was time to move to another place.
Tsityostinako said she would show them the way.
Tsityostinako asked her daughters to gather the People.
Uretsiti and Naot'siti brought the People.
They brought the People to one place.

They brought the People there.
Tsityostinako told them to prepare for their journey.
The People became prepared.
The People prepared for four days.
Tsityostinako, Uretsiti, and Naot'siti sang through the night.
The song was sung until morning.
This was the fourth morning.
Tsityostinako, Uretsiti, and Naot'siti joined together.

Their union created a *h'a-ak* [Douglas spruce] seed.
They planted *h'a-ak* in song.
The *h'a-ak* was fertilized by the rain in song.
The seed grew strong in mother earth as they sang.
The stem punctured the seed skin as they sang.
The stem of the tree grew upwards as they sang.
The stem held the strength of the sky as they sang.
The stem held the warmth of the earth as they sang.
The stem became a tree trunk as they sang.
The trunk of the tree grew round as they sang.
The tree trunk grew tall as they sang.
The tree grew through the Yellow World as they sang.
The singing voices carried the tree upward.
The strong tree trunk was now in the Blue-Green World.
The tree was now ready to carry life to the Upper World.
Time had come for the People to move to the Blue-Green
    World.
Tsityostinako told the People that it was time to ascend.
Tsityostinako asked Koshairi to climb first.
Koshairi climbed the tree.
Koshairi shook the tree.
Koshairi jumped on the branches of the tree.
Koshairi yelled at the tree.
Koshairi reached the top of the tree.
The song of ascension was all around Koshairi.
Koshairi was in the Blue-Green World.
Koshairi climbed back down to the People.

Koshairi told them that the tree was ready.

They started to climb the tree.
Koshairi led the People.
Then came the three mothers and all the societies.
The People went up in the order in which they had been
    created.
There were some who fell back down.
They went unnoticed.

Life was in the Blue-Green World.
They stayed for four years.
The People were fed. Naot'siti and Uretsiti nursed the People
    and they lived.
The People, animals, and life multiplied.
The Blue-Green World became crowded.
The People knew it was time to leave this place.
The time had come to move to the next place.
They did not know how they could do this.
They did not know if they could do this.
The People asked Naot'siti and Uretsiti.
They asked the sisters to show them the way.
The sisters called upon their mother.
Tsityostinako said she would show them the way.
Tsityostinako would take the People to the right Place.
Tsityostinako spoke to her daughters.
She asked them to gather the People.

Uretsiti and Naot'siti brought the People together.
They brought the People together in this one Place.
Tsityostinako asked the People to prepare.
The People prepared for the journey.
Tsityostinako and Uretsiti and Naot'siti sang.
They sang all through the night.
The song was sung until the fourth morning.
Tsityostinako, Uretsiti and Naot'siti joined together.
They joined in song.
A *henati* cloud was born from the song.
Henati dropped a tree seed as they sang.
The tree grew tall and strong with the song.

The singing helped the tree grow to the Red World.
Kwiraina was sent to try out the tree first.
Kwiraina climbed, shaking the tree.
Kwiraina jumped on the branches of the tree.
Kwiraina yelled at the tree.
The song of ascension was all around Kwiraina.
Kwiraina reached the top.
He knew that the tree was safe.
He then turned and looked about at the place.
> "This is the place my mother sent me to see,
> So I am making the tree firm for the People."
Kwiraina climbed back down the tree.
Kwiraina told Uretsiti that the tree was firm.
She thanked Kwiraina.

All things of life moved up to the Red World.
Kwiraina led the way.

There were some who fell back down.

They went unnoticed.

People lived in the Red World for four years.
There were too many in this place.
The time had come for the People to move to the next place.
They did not know if they could do this.
They did not know if there was another place.
They asked the sisters to show them the way.
The sisters called upon their mother to show them the way.
The time had come for the People to move to a higher Place.
Tsityostinako said she would show them the way.
Tsityostinako would take the People to the higher place.
Tsityostinako spoke to her daughters.
Tsityostinako told them to come.
She asked them to gather the People.
Uretsiti and Naot'siti brought the People.
They brought the People together in one place.
The sisters and the People came to Tsityostinako.

Tsityostinako asked the People to prepare for the journey.
The People prepared for four days.
Tsityostinako and Uretsiti and Naot'siti sang through the
    night.

The song was sung until morning.
This was the fourth morning.
Tsityostinako, Uretsiti, and Naot'siti joined together in song.
The People performed ceremonies.
The Elders watched the children.
The younger men and women guarded sacred places of
    ceremony.
That is what they were taught to do.
Then they sang the songs.
They sang in their strength.
They sang with their unity.
They sang as they were taught.
The *heyoc* tree was made from seed.
They sang.
It grew faster than any of the other trees.
They sang.
The *heyoc* tree moved through difficult places.

They sang.
The song bent around the tree.
They sang.
The *heyoc* tree grew.
The song pushed through hard dirt and rock.
Koshairi was told to climb the *heyoc* tree.
Koshairi was told to climb this tree.
Koshairi climbed out of sight.

Koshairi returned,
    "The tree is blocked. It cannot get through the hard rock."
The song stopped.
Uretsiti called on Dyupi Moti, Badger Boy.
Dyupi Moti climbed up the *heyoc* tree.
The People sang.

Dyupi Moti came to the hard rock surface.
The People sang.
Dyupi Moti started digging.
The People sang.
Dyupi Moti opened the rock.
The People sang.
The *heyoc* tree moved through the hole.
The People sang.
Dyupi Moti climbed back down the tree.
He climbed down to the singing People.
Uretsiti was told of the opening.
Dyupi Moti told Uretsiti,
      "Some of the rocks are sharp.
      People will get hurt on the sharp rocks."
Uretsiti sent for Tsika Moti.
Tsika Moti made noises like cicada.
The People sang.
Tsika Moti made sharp rocks smooth.
The People sang.

Tsika Moti came back down.
The People sang.
Tsika Moti told the mother of the smooth rocks.
The People climbed the tree.
These trees are known as ladders.
The People climbed up to the next world.
Some fell back down.
They went unnoticed.
The People reached the White World.
They liked it.
They decided to live here in this Place.
The People thanked Naot'siti, Uretsiti, and Tsityostinako.
The Ya-ya mother thanked them.
They said that they would live here long.
The People settled.
Life took its place.
The People sang.

In this place they learned of harmony.
Then, there was a loud noise which came from behind them.
Uretsiti wondered who was making that noise.
She turned to see.
The People turned around to see.
Hododo came up.

Wikori came up.
They had fallen back down.
No one had noticed.
They were the fathers.
They were angry.
They were moving with great force.
They were throwing rocks up out of their way.

They were shooting up fire out of their way.
They were shaking the dirt out of their way.
Four points of their horns came up first.
The Hododo were very strong.
The Wikori were very strong.

They lifted their four points high in the air.

Uretsiti knew the four points.
The four points were the deer horns.
Uretsiti asked the Hododo,
    "Why have you fallen behind? You are strong yet you come
    last. Why?"
The Hododo grumbled.
The Wikori grumbled.
The Hododo spoke,
    "We can do anything with these horns. We can pierce
    anything with these horns. We can do magic with these
    horns."

The Wikori spoke,
    "These horns are very heavy to carry, and while they could
    be considered a burden, we chose to carry them. We have

come with these heavy horns of importance. We have come at last. Now we are here."

Uretsiti said,

"Hereafter, you shall be the way you are now. You shall cause the land to shake and tremble with these horns. You shall have the power to pass through anything. You shall always be as you are, for you hold magical power as is the *ianyi*, but your *ianyi* shall be limited in its power."

The Hododo relaxed.

The Wikori relaxed.

Uretsiti spoke,

"This place of emergence is to be called K'a'tsi Kadawei, the Earth's navel. This is the place of balance and harmony, the healing place."

Here we are in this place.

Uretsiti told the People,

"The earth is the body. The navel holds us to our Mother, and the Shipap is the place where creation took place, down in the fourth world, the place of germination."

The Hododo carried the horns from the Shipap before the deer were created. The Wikori and the Hododo became known as the wise grandfathers who held the power of the animals and the wisdom of the ages.

The People were shown how to build a *pa'eima*, a place to live, near the navel. The People then became curious and started to migrate. They moved toward the south, building a *pa'eima* as they moved. Each one of these temporary dwelling areas was given a name.

Kacikatcutiya, White-House Place, was the last of the pueblos built before the People reached their present location. Uretsiti told the People that they had to live here, for they could not return to the lower worlds. The men grew food, wheat, beans, melons, and other crops. Uretsiti created seeds of all kinds for them to plant. When the plants were young, strong, and growing, the tcaiyani performed ceremonies to keep the plants strong.

The Shiwana [Katsina-singers] brought the rain.

Everyone believed what he was taught.
Everyone did as he was told.
Everyone had a good life.
　　It rained almost every day.

　　Tsityostinako let her presence be known through wisdom taught in dreams.
　　The importance of ritual was given to each person.
　　Each person learned of his or her role, custom, and needs, in order to make the spirits listen, care, and continue to bring what was needed to survive.

3. Ololowishka

Uretsiti and Naot'siti brought forth the Priest That Holds the Six Man-Healing Fetishes for Fertilization. This priest, named Ololowishka, was one of the Rain Makers.

There was a distinction between medicine ceremonials and ceremonials for rain. For the latter ceremony, the healer needed the sacred-shell mixture. The ceremonial sacred shell had to go through the purification, as well as the men using it. They were to bathe and have their heads washed in yucca suds—a form of physical purification.

The ceremonies themselves were of the same type as planting rites that came between the rain ceremonials. The sacred shell was washed in the rain; the men bathed in the river filled with the rain; and the fruition of life continued with that germination from the Sky Father.

Ololowishka was the spirit of germination that entered into the healer who danced and gave respect to the Great Mother/Father Tsityostinako.

Tsityostinako told him how to perform his role:

"You are to be the representative of the sky water. You are to sweeten bread by letting the sweet water from your body fall upon the corn meal. Your waters will represent the waters that fall from Sky Father. Make a gourd to carry before you in place of where your organ is. Let forth water from the gourd, water sweetened by honey and yucca fruits. Let that which is sweet and rich fall upon the harvested corn meal."

Tsityostinako then gave the Koi Shiwanni [dance leader] his instructions:

"Ololowishka is to hold in his left hand a hoop on which a yellow bird is perched. In his right hand he is to hold a crooked stick. The stick shall point to a woman who will stand next to Ololowishka. The woman shall hold a stick in her right hand. Her stick shall cross Ololowishka's stick. The woman's stick will have a yellow bird with black wings standing on it. This is done in respect for Uretsiti, who brought many birds to help guide the People from the sacred *manta*.

"Ololowishka shall paint his body black. The woman shall be painted yellow. Ololowishka shall only wear a wide belt holding two rainbow symbols setting out in direction to the hoop. The gourd organ shall come out from below the belt, held low with leather.

"The woman shall wear only a sash around her waist, from which long fringe shall hang down. The woman should wear soft sandals. Ololowishka and the woman shall be painted about the face. The cheek of each shall have a warrior symbol painted on it. At the feet of each shall be placed items of respect. Ololowishka shall have a bow and two arrows. The woman will have a burden basket with a yellow bird on it. Four flute players shall stand at the sides of the grinding stones. Young girls shall take their corn kernels and kneel, grinding corn at the grinding stones. Young girls shall take their corn kernels and kneel, grinding corn at the grinding stones. The flute players shall sing the grinding song. When the song is finished, the flute players will help the young girls stand, each carrying their bowls of corn meal.

"You, the leader, will say, 'Hurry up, children, your grandfather wishes to bring the waters of life to you.' The bowls will be taken from the young girls and set down in front of Ololowishka. Ololowishka will carry the long-necked gourd in his hand in front. He will stand over the bowl and pour some of his liquid into it.

"Then he will go to the second bowl and do the same. You, as the leader, shall put your hands into the bowl, mix the contents thoroughly, and carry the bowls around among the People; and the People will take some of the corn meal from the bowls.

"The young girls will rise. They are to dance the Corn Dance, each holding an ear of corn.

"Ololowishka then shall call any men who are holding sicknesses in their bodies, and Ololowishka will cure them. Ololowishka shall keep men from disease or evil, and he shall cure them so that they will not make their women sick.

"Ololowishka shall never be seen except at this particular ceremony."

Ololowishka brought the rain, and the plants grew, the People healed, and life was good.

The plants grew, and when the squash were ripe the People gathered them. They were shown how to keep them. They were told how to prepare them. They were shown how to give thanks. The People continued to learn, to grow, and to nurture the land.

The land changed with the growing.

The crops of some were better than the crops of others.

The changing of the crops brought about confusion. The People were no longer equal. Some had better crops than others and, therefore, had more wealth. The People started fighting. The divisions of the family were painful. Death meant weakness, and the weaknesses of the dead were passed on to the living.

4. Macta-hotcanyi

Death then had to be controlled. If one person killed many, that one person then contained the weakness of all those he had killed. This would bring about terrible illness, and, if he was not purified, would bring illness and death to those with whom he communicated.

The sacred sister Uretsiti saw that her people were not having good or healthy lives. She decided to create an overseer who would control the killing and purification of the People:

Macta-hotcanyi was created first. His duties were those of the War Chief. Macta-hotcanyi took from others, so Uretsiti turned him into a wood rat. Opi-hotcanyi was then Warrior Chief. Altars were made to send prayers to the sky spirits.

Sun Father spoke to the People:

"Nearby, in the corn priests' court,
Our two fathers (the twin war gods),
The ones who hold the high places,
With all their sacred things,
Made their roads of color enter.
There from all sides,
Those who are our fathers,
All the water-bringing birds,
Pekwin's Priests,
Made their roads come forth.
They made their roads of color come hither.
With his hand,
With his heart...."

The rainbow tells of the Cloud People. Rainbow provides the Cloud People a way down to this world. Rainbow is used as a shrine to the War Gods. Rainbow, or *Amitolan,* arcs from the mouth of the great Eagle.

The Rainbow comes forth from the great Eagle. The great Eagle brings fatness, firmness, and moisture to the corn kernels.

The corn kernels thus provide the necessary food and give sustenance to the People, who no longer need to kill and take from others.

5. Sacred Sisters

The Tanoan people traveled the land, learning of life, death, birth, and harmony. With this, however, came the awareness of war. War brings a disease that goes on for generations. This disease carries from father to son, mother to daughter, tribe to tribe; and with the myth comes the awareness that this was not the way it always was. No, not at all. This came about from an anger that was felt long ago. When the anger was recognized, and the pain that arose from such anger made apparent to the children, they could begin to heal the tribe, the family, and the way of the land. This is the story of war, the birth of war, from two sisters who were never allowed to work together too closely.

To know this story is to be forewarned. When one knows how to avoid illness, death, sorrow, and disharmony, one remains healthy.

The first people lived in an underground world. It was dark, crowded, and filled with bodies.

They came up from the Shipap [place of emergence], in the north, over there, from that peak. The mother/father of these beings was called Uresete. She was the first mother/father of those who were not ready yet or those who did not know The Way of Respect and Honor.

Uresete had one son, Ma'a sewi. Uresete sent him to find the sun. He found it in white earth, staying in one of the four-corner directions. After Uresete and Ma'a sewi put Sun in the place of the east, Ma'a sewi became the leader and brought the People up into the light to the White-House Place.

Uresete let Gopher dig, for the People were slow and confused. The all-creator Tsityostinako gave Uresete a basket with

sides and their images at the cardinal points. Uresete was told to plant four pine seeds, and Badger came up, then Locust. Each came to life from his own image.

Then Uresete gave birth to two daughters. The daughters were life forms that came from the bisexual creator Uresete, who took a clot of her own blood and threw it to the earth, making the sisters. The birth was one of power. The two sisters had their own names; some called them Uretsiti and Naot'siti. They sang the creation song and prayed to the sun. The sisters were taught by Spider Mother, Tsityostinako [or Sussistinako, if referred to as a male] and her helper, who had only one ear and also was a spider.

The sisters called each other by their names only. The People were united as one. Uresete, the mother and father as one, asked the sisters if the People could leave the White House. Naot'siti was angered at being asked to leave. She told her sister that she was the better one, that her people were the stronger ones, and that she wanted to have this land, in this place, for her people. Naot'siti told her sister to take *her* people back to the under-world because they were weak and useless.

Younger Sister Uretsiti said, "Let us have a competition. Whoever wins can stay in this place, but the other must move." They decided to ask Mother Uresete if they could do this. Uretsiti agreed and said, "Whomever Sun shines on first tomorrow is the stronger."

Naot'siti and Uretsiti both got up at dawn and stood waiting for Sun. Sun rose, and, since Uretsiti was taller than her elder sister, he shone on her hair first. When the light of Sun had completely covered Uretsiti, the shadow had not yet begun on Naot'siti.

When Naot'siti saw her sister standing in full sun, she was filled with anger. "Why is it that you are covered with sun while I am still in the dark?" she asked.

Uretsiti spoke softly: "You asked for this trial. Our creator has done this to show that the power was given to me to lead my people here."

Naot'siti called her people to her, and, after a great discussion, it was decided that another testing would be done.

Tsityostinako called down to the sisters and told them to put their testing aside, for it was time to plant tobacco.

The creator taught the People through the sacred sisters how to roll the corn husk and smoke the tobacco. The sisters showed the People how to make baskets. Out of the first basket came the field mouse, who is held as a great-spirit-healer holder even today.

The sisters brought life to fish and to other animals such as the piñon jay, chaparral jay, magpie, lizard, and the magical snake that came to life on its own, the Pishu'ni.

After this was accomplished, the sisters continued in their quarrel. Uretsiti and Naot'siti agreed to try a guessing game. Uretsiti gathered some birds while her sister was talking with her people. Uretsiti hid the birds in a cave. Naot'siti agreed to go into the cave and to find or guess the names of the four birds. If Naot'siti could do this, then she was the stronger.

Naot'siti entered the cave, and, not hearing the birds or finding any tracks, she guessed in anger. Her answers were wrong. Uretsiti called the birds out of the cave and proved her sister wrong in front of all the People. The birds were the wild turkey, the piñon jay, the magpie, and the roadrunner.

Naot'siti called her people to her, and they told her that it was time to test her younger sister. Naot'siti and Uretsiti agreed to cook a feast. They cooked the meat of buffalo, deer, elk, antelope, and turkey, as well as corn, bread, baked pumpkins, and corn-wheat cakes. The People were divided equally and asked to eat.

By not eating all of a sister's food, they would choose the winner, for she would be the one who had cooked the most and was the most competent to lead. The food that Naot'siti cooked was eaten quickly, while the food that Uretsiti fixed was still plentiful.

Tsityotinako called to the sisters, telling them to stop their competition. Naot'siti walked away from her sister. Laughingly, she called back, "You are not fit!"

Uretsiti ignored her sister and started back to her own people. Naot'siti, now in a rage, turned and leaped on her sister,

hitting her and punching her. Uretsiti called for her people to save her.

"Help!" she cried. "My sister wishes to kill me unfairly!"

The people of Uretsiti came and pulled Naot'siti off her. Uretsiti told her people to tie Naot'siti, naked, to a tall tree, and they did as she said.

Then Uretsiti pulled a tail feather from a turkey and cut off the breast of her older sister. The white milk that was once contained in the firm, fat breast of Naot'siti turned to red blood as it seeped into the ground at her feet. Uretsiti then cut deeper into her sister's chest and pulled out her sister's heart. Uretsiti bit off large pieces of her sister's heart and spit them upon the ground. They turned into wood rats and scampered off to the west to become the Other People, guided by Naot'siti. Uretsiti bit into the center of her sister's heart to find that it was made of cactus. The cactus needles hurt Uretsiti's mouth. Writhing in pain, Uretsiti then declared war between her people and the Other People.

War and the birth of a new disease—blind anger—had now come about. War chiefs and officers now had the role of *preventing* anger and war. People asked their permission to practice ceremonies, healing techniques, and curings.

6. Raven

Raven was known by the Hudson Bay Eskimo as Raven Man. While others were collecting their property in preparation to move, Raven Man would call out to them, reminding them that they had forgotten to bring the blankets of deerskin used for the beds. This special deerskin blanket protected the people from the dampness that would seep up into the main bedding at night. The old ones, children, the ill, and the bedridden people kept their health with these important deerskin protective blankets.

The deerskin blanket, in the Eskimo language, is called the **Kak.** *The story follows that one Raven Man called to the people to get their Kak, not to forget their Kak, many times. He raced back and forth getting the deerskin Kak for the others who were thoughtless, and the Raven Man became a raven. Ravens still fly over the people when they prepare to move and call out to them, "Kak, Kak, Kak." This is to remind them of the special deerskin blanket.*

Raven also carried the sacred sticks that started fires for sacred ceremonies.

Raven lived with the Eskimo. He took fire sticks and put them into the belly of the whale cow, for he was tired of flying and was in need of finding another method of travel. He found, within the belly of the whale cow, an entrance to a fine room. At the end of this fine room burned a lamp. Next to the lamp was a beautiful woman. The woman was more beautiful than the raven could believe. She held beauty in each of the lines in her face, in each of the tips of her fingers. Her breath floated like a soft, white cloud from her perfectly formed lips. Her breast rose and fell with each breath, and the roundness of her arms and shoulders brought raven into the room to be with this woman.

The room was dry and clean, and its ceiling was held up by the whale's spine. The ribs of the whale cow were the walls. The tube that ran along the backbone dripped oil slowly down onto the lamp and kept it lit. The sweet smell of the oil relaxed Raven as he sat down at the table opposite her. She lifted her oval-brown eyes and studied him.

Raven opened his mouth and made his sound. The woman looked up and said, "How did you get in here? You are the first of all men to enter this room."

Raven tried to clear his throat and speak with a voice of authority, but his voice was taken by this woman's beauty. He rasped out an explanation of how he had used his fire sticks. The woman studied him as he spoke. The very depth of his feelings were being pulled from him as she listened, sucking the breath from Raven's body.

Raven did not know that this woman was the very soul of the whale cow. She placed her hands on the table before her. She lifted her body slowly as she turned away from Raven. He studied this graceful body that brought to him a plate of food. She placed the meal before Raven. She gave him berries and oil. Her body gently sat down across the table from him. Her dark, red lips formed perfect words as she told him of how she had gathered berries the year before this. Raven stayed for four days as the guest of the whale cow's spirit, or Inua.

Inua herself did not stay with Raven all the time. She would listen to him, as the whale was dormant and quiet. When she grew restless, she would leave, and the whale would leap and spin in the waters of the deep. Raven got worried when this happened. Sometimes the beautiful woman did not come back for days. Sometimes she would stay for many hours and watch him. She would suck in his breath and leave him weak.

In his solitude, Raven became curious. He was fascinated by the tube running along the top of the room that fed the lamp with oil. He tried to get the Inua to tell him about this tube, but she would not respond to his question. On one occasion as she left, she warned him that he was not to touch anything in the room.

Raven walked over to the lamp, stretched out his talon, and caught a big drop of the oil. He licked it.

The oil was sweet tasting. He enjoyed it thoroughly and took more and more. Scarcely had he taken four tastes when he felt the sudden rolling of the whale cow. He wanted more. This time he broke off a piece of the tube and ate it. When he did this, a great gush of oil poured into the room. The lamp went out, and the room itself began to roll back and forth. This continued for four days, until Raven was almost dead with the rolling. He could not sleep or rest a moment for fear of falling into something that could hurt him.

Finally, the movement stopped. The room became still. Raven had broken one of the heart arteries of the whale cow. Raven had killed the whale cow. The Inua did not come back to life. She was dead, her body washed ashore to rot.

Raven now was trapped. He could not get out of the dead whale cow. He was thinking of what to do when he heard two men talking. They were walking on the back of the dead whale cow, talking about carving and carrying the meat to their village. Soon, they had cut a hole in the upper body of the great whale. The people were starving, and this dead whale cow was the food that they had prayed for and dreamed of to save themselves. When the hole was large enough for the people to enter, they carried off the pieces of meat to a higher shore. Raven quickly stepped out unnoticed.

No sooner had he walked upon the ground than he remembered that his sacred fire sticks were still inside this whale cow. He took off his coat and mask. He became a tiny black man. He was wrapped in part of the whale-cow's skin. He was a very strange-looking person. The people were unsure of him, and they backed away. He walked up to the whale cow, pulled out his sharp knife, and began to cut away at the meat. The people watched, finding him very unusual.

After a time, one of the people, who had gone into the whale cow to remove the fatty tissue, came out yelling, "Look, look what I have found! These are fire sticks. They were in the belly of the whale cow!"

Raven Man began clicking his tongue (as only a Raven Man can do). He said, "This is very bad. One time when I found fire sticks in a whale, my daughters died. This means that many people will die. This is not good. This is not good. This is not good. This is not good." Raven Man continued to click his tongue.

Raven Man dropped his knife and began to run away. He called out as he ran, "If you treasure your life and the lives of your family, you will run from these fire sticks!"

Raven Man moved swiftly away from the dead whale cow. The people followed him, not knowing what to believe, but expecting the worst. Raven Man doubled back and picked up his fire sticks. He then sat down and feasted on the whale cow all by himself.

7. Maple Sugar and Menstruation

The Menomini Indians lived during a time when Ma'nabush, the great hero, returned empty -handed from a hunting trip. This was most depressing, for both he and his grandmother were hungry. Ma'nabush was a great hero, and for him to return with no food was humiliating. He was also very hungry.

He went home to his grandmother, and they decided to move to another place where perhaps the game was more plentiful. His grandmother was most hopeful, saying that the animals were respectful of Ma'nabush and had moved to another area. They spoke of other places they could go. They gathered together all their things. After traveling a long distance, they built a new wig'i'wam among the trees. Grandmother's name was Noko'mis. Noko'mis studied the trees and called them maples.

Noko'mis told Ma'nabush, "Grandson, we will not go hungry now. You do some simple tasks and let your grandmother feed you. If you will go into the woods and gather some birchbark for me, I am going to make sugar."

Ma'nabush went into the woods. He gathered up strips of birchbark and took these back to Noko'mis at the wig'i'wam. Noko'mis already had some other bark, and with it she sewed together pieces of birchbark to make containers for the sugar.

Noko'mis went from maple to maple, cutting small holes in the trunk of each tree and inserting small pieces of wood over which the sap ran into containers. Ma'nabush followed his grandmother from tree to tree. He watched her and appreciated her patience. He saw only her work and did not believe that the sap would fall into the containers.

Noko'mis went from tree to tree and cut holes for as many containers as she had made. Ma'nabush went back and looked into the containers and saw that all of them had become half full of thick syrup. Ma'nabush put his finger into the syrup and tasted it. It was delicious.

He spoke to Noko'mis: "Grandmother, this is good, but it will not do to have these trees make sugar so easily. The people will come and do this, and it will be too easy for them. This must be more difficult. Let them come and boil the tree bark for several days and nights. Make it more difficult or soon it will all be gone."

Noko'mis smiled at him. Ma'nabush noticed that his grandmother was all dressed up and that her hair was fixed very nicely. Ma'nabush asked her, "Have you had company while I was gone?" Grandmother smiled and told him that she just wanted to get dressed nicely. Ma'nabush was worried for her.

The next morning, Ma'nabush went out hunting. He left his grandmother sleeping on her mat. When he returned that night, she was dressed up very nicely and her hair was fixed as if for a ceremony. Ma'nabush asked her, "Have you had company today?" Grandmother was busy with her herbs and said nothing.

This went on for three days, and on the fourth day, Ma'nabush decided to circle back and find out what was going on with Grandmother. Soon, Bear came into view. Waddling from side to side, he walked directly to the wig'i'wam and went in.

Ma'nabush got a piece of dried bark and lit one end of it. He made a fierce blaze, went into the doorway of the wig'i'wam, and pulled aside the covers. There he saw Bear with his grandmother. Ma'nabush threw the burning bark at Bear, and it struck him on the back just above the loin. Bear was frantic with pain. He rushed out of the opposite door of the wig'i'wam and raced for the stream in the woods.

Before Bear reached the water, flames burned the hair from his back; and, because the bark was still sticking to his body, Bear fell down dead.

After Ma'nabush threw the blazing bark at Bear, he ran from the wig'i'wam to hide in the brush. There he saw Bear racing through the woods. Ma'nabush hid and watched until Bear was dead. He took up the carcass and dragged it to the wig'i'wam.

He threw the body down on the floor next to his grandmother, saying, "There, Grandmother, I have killed a bear. Now we shall eat."

Grandmother asked, "How did you kill him?"

Ma'nabush could not tell his grandmother that he had burned him to death. So he just said, "Bear is dead. I killed him, and he is dead. Let us eat him."

Grandmother shook her head. "I cannot eat him," she said. "He was my man, my man for life."

Ma'nabush cut up Bear and offered a piece of the meat to his grandmother. Grandmother shook her head again. "That was my man," she repeated. Ma'nabush took a clot of Bear's blood and threw it at his grandmother. He hit her on the abdomen with it, saying, "There, you want your man? There, take that!"

Grandmother took the blood clot off her abdomen and held it up to Ma'nabush. "For that rude action, your aunts will have trouble every full moon and will give birth to clots just like this!"

Ma'nabush ate all the Bear meat he wanted and put the rest aside for another time. But what his grandmother promised came to pass.

8. The Old Children

There are illnesses that cannot be explained or cured. They come about from something that was not meant to be. These occurrences can actually develop into wisdom that will then protect others from making the same mistake. There is a reason for wisdom and healing. There also is a reason for listening and following the words of the wise.

There were two who were kept separate from the other people. No one can remember why these two were separated. The woman was devoted to her man. When her man would sit thoughtfully and wonder on life, his woman would sit quietly and wonder with him. When the man was happy and would sing, the woman would sing with him. They were put apart for some reason but chose to follow their feelings rather than the wisdom of the elders.

These two bore twelve children. The woman carried each child as if it were her first. Her man took care of her and washed her tenderly before and after each birth. He met her every need and was respectful of her as his woman and the mother of his children.

The children were not like those who came before!

The children were neither male nor female. The firstborn was beautiful and graceful as a fine woman but held the strength and brawn of a man. The children were called *hlahmon,* being both man and woman, combined as a seed with two hearts, ripened as both, not one.

The oldest was considered to be a female, and she was given the name of a female. She held within her the seeds of life, and she ripened with time.

Her brothers, as the other eleven were called, bore only a semblance of males. The fruit within them was not of passion. Their organs grew but not with the power of being males. They had bodies that were firm, muscular, and manly, but they were dun-colored with welts. They acted like simpletons and spoke much like a wise man speaks to his followers.

They were named. Their names were not names of men but names of mismeaning. First there was Pekwina, the Priest-speaker of the Sun. He was thoughtful, even in the heat of the day, and spoke out of turn if he felt the need to speak.

The second was named Pi'hlan Shiwani, for he held the knowledge of the Bow-Priest warrior. He spent most of his time hiding behind trees, frightened of even the fluttering of a leaf.

The third was named Eshotsi, after the bat. This one saw better than anyone in the bright sunlight. His vision did little to help him, for he would hurt himself on his shadow and would run from a hole in the ground or a place where he was not looking clearly.

The fourth was named Mauiyapona, or Wearer of the Eyelets of Invisibility. This one had horns like a catfish and was born with knobs on his body like a squash. His ugliness frightened him; yet when he hid, he hid only his head, leaving the rest of him to be seen by all who would pass.

The fifth was Potsoki, or the Pouter. He did little else but laugh and look bland. He tried to hide his lack of thought with laughter, but his laughter only echoed his emptiness. His younger brothers were:

- Na'hlashi, or the Aged Buck, the Biggest of All. He cried and cried and cried and cried, rubbing his eyes until there were large droopy bags of skin hanging down under them like a toad.

- Frisky as a Fawn, who giggled like a girl and never could work, for this one was always running away to pretend.

- Carried Off, who was carried off by the Snail of the South before they could find out who he was and give him a name that would not fit him.

- Itseposa, or the Glum, who mourned continuously for his older brother who had been carried off by the Snail of the South. He cried until his eyes were dry and his chin chapped to protrusion. Yet this one pushed to live cheerfully and tried to be compliant.

- K'ya'lutsi, or the Suckling, and his twin Tsa'hlashi, the Old Youth.

The twins were the most important, for they were always advising the others and strutting about like young priests at their first dance. Yet their knowledge was too old, and they never learned to grow, for they were born old, too old ever to be young.

The father stood dazed with his head bowed and his hands clasped before him, like broken bows hanging from his side, while he watched the children romp and play. The Wise Ones said that these children were Ka'yemashi, or the Spirits of the Sacred Drama Dance, who would teach the people to follow the traditional rules. Spirits would play with those who did not listen.

These children became spirits. They offered lessons and were noted for their strange behavior. Those who are different have great spirit, for they hold the wisdom of the spirits that teach the way of the people. The rules of life are to be obeyed or consequences will follow that cannot be healed or corrected but must be lived with, good or bad.

Chants

Many interested readers ask if there is more information regarding the chant-stories. The purpose of the stories is not just to relay data but to bring certain feelings.

Native-American Pueblo people feel the story is different for each listener. Each moment of every day is a religious experience. Life is lived in the present, and the feeling of the present helps one grow toward the future. The past is over, and there is nothing one can do about it.

*These stories of healing relate to the way of the **beginning**, which is not the past per se. The beginning holds the knowledge of what we need to know now. Stories in the past tense are felt now as they are told or read. How one feels currently can change as one progresses, but the feeling should heal what once was not seen or felt. Through feelings such as anger, we wander off our true path. To recognize those feelings, hear those feelings, feel those feelings, will help us realize that we are (or are not) on the path of harmony.*

Healing stories are heard from the outside, and to elevate their influence, many Native Americans use chants. A chant allows the outside voice to penetrate one's being, to bring a hypnotic balance of the spirit. The story of the chant does not hold the power; but the vibration of the chant, felt deeply, internally, moves one from within.

*To say that out of logic comes healing would, in the way of the People, be a misconception. Logic works on logical situations; spirit feeling works on spirit. Harmony brings disharmony into balance, and the vibrations of the chant bring the spirit from a faraway place into the center. The resonating sounds, the nasal pitch, the glottal short stops, the long methodical repeating—all these move the internal chant into a place of balance. The chant need not make sense; the purpose of it is to **Feel.***

Feel the chant. Let the healing come from within you. The chant will bring balance, healing, and harmony.

1. Medicine of the Old Ones

In the southern pueblos, the old ones talk of a time when the people were believed to have two hearts, one good and one evil. If a person did bad deeds, the bad heart had overwhelmed the good heart. The patient with a bad heart was known as a *kana' Dyaiya,* which the missionaries translated as "witch." These people were believed to hold "traffic with evil." They were associated with owls and crows, and it was thought they could transform themselves into coyotes, burros, or wood rats. Anyone could be a witch and could keep it a secret.

Medicine people had the power to kill witches, oppose evil, and cure people. They received this virtue through the power of animal-healing spirits. The greatest spirit power came from the bear, and medicine healers wore bear-claw necklaces and the skins of the forelegs of bears on their arms when they treated patients. The badger also was a great medicine-holder spirit. He held strength because he dug in the ground and knew the cures of roots. The eagle, snake, and shrew were considered powerful doctors as well. Indian medicine men obtained their power from these wise animals by means of songs or chanting.

Native Americans have a primary deity place, the Place of the Great Spirit, and the Great Spirit has other spirits to help in healing. The natural state of life is whole, in total harmony. The healing chants and ceremonies bring about the restoration of wholeness, for disease is a condition of disharmony or of separateness within. Beauty is wholeness or harmony. Health is wholeness or harmony. Goodness, purity, and success are being whole.

The circle of being is not a physical state, but, rather, a dynamic state of harmony. This healthy harmony comes from within and lives, moves, knows, acknowledges true life—greater life. Acknowledgement of this greater life allows healing chants to heal and to make the sick person well again.

In the natural, healthy state, one is related to all life, to all phenomena, to all things of this earth and all of the cosmos and Great Spirits beyond. The chant heals through the resonating of the soul.

2. K'a'nashku'le

This story is told in rhythm. The repetition serves to quiet childish psychological temperaments and assures that each person is exerting spiritual internal energy to overcome external phenomena. The repetition of the chant elevates one out of delusion and achieves union with the Great Spirit. This union allows the ceremony to produce certain results such as healing, bringing rain, or ensuring that natural events move in their accustomed way so they will bring prosperity to the person and the community.

A long time ago,
K'a'nashku'le was living underground and
he wanted white skin. His skin was dark,
dark as the blackness that he lived in.
He took off his black, like a shirt.
He was then white and pink at the same time.
He wanted to see the sunshine,
but he had no eyes.
He spoke four times.
When he spoke, he died.
The next time he spoke, a cricket came to him.
The second time he spoke, he became a living person.
The third time he spoke, he had dark skin.
The fourth time he spoke, his skin was black.
He decided to come up when it was summer.
It was too hot.
It became cold.
Someone saw him moving slowly.
The people killed him.
It was believed that he could not die,

but went back down to the underworld.
He called to white worm.
White worm was asked to carry K'a'nashku'le
to the above world.
K'a'nashku'le rode the white worm to this place
and he called out to be one of the people.
They would not accept him, for he was all black as the earth.
He was black as the clouds that carry water.
The people would not let him stay.
K'a'nashku'le rode the white worm home to the underworld.
K'a'nashku'le changed his skin to white.
K'a'nashku'le called to white worm.
K'a'nashku'le received advice from cricket.
K'a'nashku'le rode white worm up to this place.
K'a'nashku'le was rubbed by the dirt and his black shown
        through.
K'a'nashku'le let the people laugh at him.
K'a'nashku'le was sad and rode the white worm back to the
        underworld.
White worm carried K'a'nashku'le back to the place of his
        fathers.
White worm and cricket told K'a'nashku'le to stay in the un-
        derworld.
K'a'nashku'le painted his body again and called to white
        worm.
K'a'nashku'le covered his body with dirt mud.
K'a'nashku'le rode the white worm.
The mud wore off K'a'nashku'le, but he stayed white.
The people laughed at him for now they knew of his tricks.
K'a'nashku'le was sad.
K'a'nashku'le died.
K'a'nashku'le was not dead for long.
K'a'nashku'le rode white worm to the underworld.
The people felt badly about hurting K'a'nashku'le's feelings.
They made an altar for him and showed respect to
        K'a'nashku'le.
The people asked K'a'nashku'le to bring the rain.
The people asked K'a'nashku'le to call to the Cloud People.

The people asked K'a'nashku'le to bring the Lightning People.
The people asked K'a'nashku'le to bring the moisture from
    Sky Father.
K'a'nashku'le brought the rain.
He still rides white worm in the underworld.
K'a'nashku'le stayed in the underworld and is thankful that
    the people remember him.
He answers their prayers when they chant.
He sends them good health with his dew.
He sends them good health with his rain.

The Cloud People and the Cloud Spirits are still called upon to heal many illnesses, including lightning shock. The Cloud People cleanse the earth with their rain water; they wash away evil with their pure rain water; and they feed the plants with their rain water.

3. Sikas'sige

The ceremony may or may not be performed anymore, but the medicine drawing by the chief of Mide', Sikas'sige, at Mille Lacs in 1830 still holds the original story.

Sikas'sige told the story in his place of residence at the White Earth; and it has been written, told, and carried since that time. This is the story that was told to me.

In the beginning, before the First Ones were here, Dzhe Man'ido made the Mide' Man'idos [First Ones]. Dzhe Man'ido created two men and two women. They had no power of thought or reason. Dzhe Man'ido made them thoughtful. Dzhe Man'ido made them feel. He took them in his strong hands so that they would multiply. He placed them in pairs, and from the pairs came the Indians. The people were placed upon the earth. He saw that they were subject to sickness, misery, and death. He needed to provide them with Sacred Medicine.

Dzhe Man'ido was divided from the earth by four lesser spirits. Dzhe Man'ido decided to talk with them, and he asked them the mysteries by which the Indians could be saved. Dzhe Man'ido first spoke to the spirit closest to him. He told him all that he had to say. Dzhe Man'ido waited. Dzhe Man'ido waited awhile longer. Dzhe Man'ido waited.

Dzhe Man'ido then spoke to the spirit who was second down from him. He told him all that he had to say. Dzhe Man'ido waited. Dzhe Man'ido waited awhile longer. Dzhe Man'ido waited.

Dzhe Man'ido then spoke to the spirit who was third away from him. He told him all that he had to say. He waited. Dzhe Man'ido waited awhile longer. Dzhe Man'ido waited.

Dzhe Man'ido then spoke to the spirit who was fourth away from him and the one closest to the earth. He told him all that he had to say. They all met in council.

They called the four wind gods to come to the consultation. After consulting as to what would be best for the care, nurturing, and welfare of the people, the spirits agreed to ask Dzhe Man'ido to communicate the Mystery of the Sacred Medicine to them. Dzhe Man'ido followed the advice of the council and went to the Sun Spirit, asking him to go to the earth and instruct the people.

The Sun Spirit changed into the form of a little boy and went to earth and lived with a woman and a man who had a little boy. The fall came, and the family went to the hills to hunt. The weather turned cold and the woman's son died. The people were distressed. They decided to return to the village and bury the son. They gathered up their items to return. Each night they traveled, they erected poles upon which the body was placed to prevent animals from eating it. When the dead boy was hanging upon the poles, the adopted Sun Spirit child stayed around the camp. His adopted father was sad. His adopted mother was sad.

The adopted Sun Spirit boy went to each of the parents and told them that he felt their sorrow. He told them that he could bring his dead brother to life. The parents became excited and asked him how this could be done.

The adopted Sun Spirit boy asked the people to hurry to the village. He told them, "Women, make a wig'i'wam of bark, put the dead boy in a covering of birch bark, and place the body on the ground in the middle of the wig'i'wam." The next morning after this had been done, the family and friends went into this wig'i'wam and sat around the corpse.

They had all been sitting quietly for some time when they saw a bear coming through the door. The bear entered the wig'i'wam. He sat down before the dead son. The bear leaned back and said, "Hu, hu, hu, hu." Then he stood up and walked to the left, trembling. He continued to sing. The dead body quivered. The bear chanted four times. The body quivered again and then came to life. The bear called to the father in the distant right-hand corner of the wig'i'wam:

Nos ka-wi-na-ni-shi-na-bi wis-si a'-ya-wi-an man-i-do nin-gi-sis. Be-mai-a-mi-nik ni-dzi man-i-do mi-a-zhi-gwa tshi-gi-a-we-an. Nos a-zhi-gwa a-se-ma tshi-a-to-yek. A-mi-kun-dem mi-e-tah a-wi-dink dzhi-gosh-kwi-tot wen-dzhi-bi-mah'-di-zid-o-mah a-ga-wa bi-ma-di-zid-mi-o-ma: ni-dzi man-i-co mi-a-zhi-gwa tshi-gi-we-an.

When he finished the healing chant, he told the adopted father that he needed to return to the spirit world with a gift of tobacco for his Sun Father. He told the people the chant meant they no longer needed to fear sickness. Now that they knew the way of the Grand Medicine, this would keep them alive. He said that his spirit could bring life to the dead only once.

4. Hummingbird

The Guiana Indians tell this chant-story of the coming of tobacco.

A man lived with a woman for a long, long time. She was a beautiful woman, a patient woman, a woman who was very good at weaving hammocks. This woman, though, did not bear any children. This made the man sad. He chose to take another woman, and this second one had a baby. They were not happy.

The baby was called Kurusiwari. Kurusiwari grew quickly, and while his stepmother wove the hammocks, he would hang on the suspended cord, pulling it loose. The stepmother tried to be patient with the little one, but it was very difficult.

One day, the baby, who was now a child, became even more mischievous than usual, pulling on the cord. The stepmother said, "Go away. Go and play over there." The stepmother clenched her teeth in anger, for the son seemed more interested in getting attention than in helping her.

The boy obeyed but soon came back and hung from the cord. The stepmother did not know how to speak to this one. She now pushed the youngster away. The youngster fell and began to cry. No one noticed. No one saw the youngster crawl out of the house. The youngster's mother and father were lying together in their hammock.

It was late in the day when, finally, one of them missed the youngster. The child was nowhere to be found. The mother and father went to a neighbor's house and asked if anyone had seen the child. The neighbor said that the child had been playing with some other child down the way. The mother and father went to the other houses and asked about the child. They began talking with their neighbors, completely forgetting about their child.

They suddenly realized that not only was Kurusiwari missing, but that Matura-wari, the neighbor's child, was gone as well.

The four parents walked to another neighbor's house, looking for their children. These parents began to talk and forgot about their sons, and soon it was learned that now another child was missing. The third missing child was Kawai-wari. The parents went to another house and did the same thing. They began to talk on other things and forgot about the children.

In the meantime, the children had wandered on and on. They made friends with the *marabuntas* [wasps]. The marabuntas spoke in those days and did not sting. The children told the marabuntas to sting their parents. They told the red ones to give their parents a fever. It was the children who arrived at the seashore at the same time as the parents of Kurusiwari. The children by now were adults. They had grown in all the time that it had taken the parents to find them.

The parents were happy to see their children and asked them to return home. At this time, Kurusiwari spoke: "I cannot return. My stepmother pushed me down. I cried, and when I ran away from home, you would not even look for me. I will not go home."

The mother and father were in tears and begged him to return. It was then that they built a proper spirit house and called him into it with tobacco. This did not work, and the children never returned home. The parents all were killed by the wasps, and now parents have learned to watch their children and not to let anger allow them to push their children away.

The children who had grown became the hummingbirds that chant or sing the songs of wisdom and keep the adults patient and thoughtful.

5. The Contest

God entered a contest with one of the old Keresan Katsinas. "Let us both shoot at a tree and see who does best." So God shot with a very heavy man-made gun, but the Katsina hit the tree with lightning. The Katsina split the tree.

They discussed the best food to eat. God sat at a table with lots of good natural foods. The Katsina sat on the ground with smoked venison and freshly fried tortillas and enjoyed them so much that God came down from his chair and joined him.

Then they both decided that it was time to bring water to help with the planting of more crops. God wrote a letter asking for rain to come. But while someone was reading it, the Katsina took a prayer feather and brought down the rain from the clouds.

Next, they tried a musical contest. God blew a horn, and the Katsina sang to a drum. At last they became tired, and God went away on a cloud, while the Katsina rode on the back of a duck.

6. Hopi Cloud Swallower

When this story began, it was at Dry Lake where a man called Ash Drinker lived. There were some surrounding smaller villages, and to the east the War Gods lived with their grandmother atop Towayalane. Early one morning, while they were eating, the War Gods said, "After we finish eating, we will go fix our traps." They had hunting traps along the dry washes. Their grandmother warned, "You can go, but there is a horrible monster at the bottom of the washes. Don't you look at it or you will be turned into dust."

"If it is a monster, we will not look into its eyes!" the two War Gods told their grandmother and ran out the door of her home. They went to the edge of the washes. They looked over and saw an object big and white curled up in a ball at the bottom of the wash.

"What should we do with this?"

"Let's yell at it and let it know that we are here."

"You yell first then."

"I don't want to. You do it."

Finally, the younger brother yelled at it, and the white thing moved just a little. The big white object stood up and peered around. The brother yelled again, and the big white thing started to run. It went over the mountains in a few bounds.

Then a grandmother bear heard this and said, "Who else could be here but me? I am all alone." She stood up on her round, heavy haunches with her paws lifting in the air, and she growled. The white object turned around and headed back.

"Now, brother, it is your turn to take its life," the younger brother said. The older brother threw a turquoise weapon, and it lodged in the creature's heart. The Cloud Swallower (which is what this big white object was) fell to the ground. The weapon flew to a place by the Ash River. There was a flock of pigeons drinking, and their feathers were cut away from their legs by the turquoise weapon. That is why pigeons have naked red feet. The weapon kept moving to the place where the bears lived.

The War Gods yelled again, "If there is anyone behind the Ash River, stop our weapon! It is heading there!" The grandfather bear heard this and knelt down before the weapon as it hit him on the back. The War Gods went over and looked at the Cloud Swallower as it lay stretched out. It covered a large space. It was huge.

The grandmother approached her grandsons and asked, "Did you take its life?"

"Yes, we did and that was for the best."

She replied, "Many of our Rain Gods have gone out into the clouds and have never returned. This creature must have been the cause of their disappearance. It is not an earthly being."

She turned, saying, "From now on, when one wishes to use the bow and arrow for protection, as the Great Ones do, it will be available to them. This place shall be known as the place to ask for the blessings of the hunt. The people will plant prayer feathers here and fast to thank you for saving them from the Cloud Swallower."

"Now will you tell us what to do?" the Twin War Gods asked their grandmother as they pointed to Grandfather Bear. Grandmother said a prayer, and Grandfather Bear sat up and sang. The song was about the hunters going to Salt Lakes, cutting prayer sticks, and planting them there. This would purify the people and allow them to kill for the sake of survival.

7. Shoomehcoolie

When one is near death, it is called the time of the White
Shoomehcoolie. If the person is healed by a medicine man, then
that person can join his clan. Women who belong to this clan must
wear masks.

There was a time when the villages of Hawikuh, Hehshokda, and Kechipbowa existed. Some people of Hawikuh wished to have a ceremony to bring back the spirits of the villagers. They were a bored people and had chosen to live in quiet solitude. Many of them did not want a ceremony; after all, that would take too much energy, and they would have to interact with one another.

Those who knew how disrespectful it was not to have a ceremony called upon Yellow Ant, who dwelled in Kechipbowa. He was sought because he had a brilliant mind and was good at betting people to do things. Yellow Ant came at once to help. When he arrived, he asked why he had been asked to come to such a quiet, calm village. He was told of the people's wish to have a ceremony to bring back the life of the village. There was nothing but quiet solitude in this village, and it was deathly still. There was nothing around, no energy, no spirit, and the people needed something or they would blow away.

Yellow Ant spoke: "In four days' time, we will have a ceremony. Eight days should be set aside for it. When the first four days are here, we will call the spirits of our fathers through our offerings of prayer sticks. For four days following that, we will dance and dance."

The Bow Priests declared that the ceremony was to be held. For the next eight days, the prayer sticks were prepared. Prayer sticks for each direction of the earth were represented, also prayer sticks for sacred animals, then for the fathers of the earth, and for the spirits who brought earth all the wonders it possesses.

The innermost place in the earth sent the powerful spirit beings. They ascended upon the village plaza, where the priests all waited for the appearance of such beings. There the offerings of prayer sticks were given them, and it was announced that the dances were to start in four days. The leader to head the dancing was chosen, and the priests thought it fitting that he, Yellow Ant, be the leader of the line dancers. His female relative, Blue Girl, was to be his partner. Black Ant was chosen to help the Yellow Ant, with Turquoise Girl as his partner.

The spirit beings departed, and the villagers began their preparations. Three days passed, and the day for the dancing arrived. The dancers came out in their proper order, and the dancing started. The *Yah* dance was then performed.

From the world of the Great Spirits came the Shoomeh-coolie clan. They arrived at Hawikuh in the form of one White Shoomehcoolie, sent to perform in the dance and bringing the spirits of the Great Fathers of the earth. Several days of dancing continued, and two spirits came out of this Great White Shoomehcoolie (who was many spirits combined in one dancer). As Shoomehcoolie continued to dance in and out of the other dancers, his energy was interrupted and he became exhausted. He stepped back from the round dancers, and the leader spirit sprinkled corn meal ahead so that the Great Dancer would go directly to the Spirit World. Without warning, the Shoomeh-coolie darted out and ran into the wooded hills.

The people were very alarmed. This was not traditional; this was not the way of the dance. The dancers ran after him but could not catch him. The Spirit World sent up two Shoomehcoolies and went to Hawikuh to follow the White Shoomehcoolie Great Dancer to Shebaboolimsa [Sacred Place in the Woods] and bring him back. The White Shoomehcoolie was not yet ready to go into the Spirit World of the Great Place of Fathers.

ᵀThe spirits found the White Shoomechoolie and took him to the Spirit World. Yellow Ant, who was leading the dance now, came to life as a real Kachina; Blue Girl became a mockingbird;

and Turquoise Girl was transformed into a hummingbird. The mockingbird and the hummingbird told the people that from that day on, should anyone want to perform this dance, the leader must have the help of the birds and be happy and content with his life or great tragedy would befall the people.

It is important to note that in chanting and ceremony all forms of participation are vital. The singers do not join in with the drum but become one with the drum; all sounds are one in strength. Movement, chant, music, emotion, all work as one. The ceremony may occur in front of others who are not chanting or dancing, but their harmony is felt as participation. Participation is given by all who are there through atonement or activity—all as one, one in harmony, to heal.

8. Giant-Who-Eats-Children

In a pueblo south of Santa Fe there lived many happy families. The families were rich in abundance for they had many, many, many children. This would have been fine except that there were some who did not share in the happiness of children. These were the witches. These witches lived near the pueblo, around the pueblo, and on occasion they even went into the pueblo. But the children were the enemies of witches: children were curious; they would snoop around; and there were even times when the witches would send warnings to the people and the children would get punished for the witches' work.

The witches held council. They decided unanimously to kill the curious, bothersome children before they outgrew their territory. The witches had among them a mother witch who had a daughter. The daughter had married a fine, tall man in the pueblo, and she herself had many children. The witches decided that they would turn the husband into a giant who would eat children. Their plan was so deliciously set up that no one would know who the man was to be or how this all was going to happen.

That night, the husband came in from the fields feeling rather poorly. His wife made him some broth, and he went to bed. By morning he was dead. The family grieved his death and buried him outside of the pueblo, as was the tradition. For four days the dead husband grew and grew and grew and grew into a giant.

On the fifth day the giant came to life. He picked himself up and walked into the pueblo. He picked up one of the children who ran up to see him. He put the child in his mouth, chewed him up, and swallowed him. Giant-Who-Eats-Children walked through the pueblo, picked up all the children and ate them. Soon there were no children at all in the pueblo.

The Indian people gathered in the plaza and sang a song to Old Woman Earth, asking her to rid them of the child-eating giant.

The Indian people of the Giant clan also came. They sang songs and prayed. They placed a large basket of white grain in the center of their group. They covered this with a sacred blanket. They sang and chanted while the others sang to Old Woman Earth. The large bulk of white grain began to move. At last it took shape and appeared to be moving. The people stared at the grain, for they knew this was great magic. The shape lifted up and stood on legs. It was the spirit of Old Woman Earth. She was in the form of a giant. Old Woman Earth Giant spoke, asking, "Why am I here?"

The people sang out, "You are here to save us from Giant-Who-Eats-Children."

"I will help you," said Old Woman Earth Giant. Then she called out, "I am here."

Giant-Who-Eats-Children came to her and said, "Who are you? Let us fight!"

The two giants moved toward each other, meeting in the plaza. The Old Woman Earth Giant said, "You hit me with your club four times. I will hit you with my obsidian knife, if I am still alive."

It was agreed. Old Woman Earth stood tall as Giant-Who-Eats-Children hit her with his club. She was unaffected by the blows. Old Woman Earth Giant took her obsidian knife and slashed open Giant-Who-Eats-Children. The sun reflected off the knife, and then cactus, thorns, rocks, and children came falling out the giant's belly.

Old Woman Earth Giant pulled these out and placed a beautiful piece of turquise inside the defeated giant's belly. Giant-Who-Eats-Children recovered and walked away from the pueblo. He went to a cave by the river and fell down to sleep. Old Woman Earth Giant followed him with a bowl of white grain. She chanted to this sleeping giant, and then she herself dissolved into the earth. Giant-Who-Eats-Children became a large mound of white powder in the cave by the river.

The people still chant to keep bad giants away:

Ho-nan
Tco-zir
Ten'a
Pu-n-e
U'se
Pi'vwa'ni
Ka'la'ci-au-u

Ko-kya-na
He'k-pa
Yun-ya
Teu'a
He'wi
Pi'h-tea

9. Ani-Tsa'guhi Bear Chants

The Ani-Tsa-guhi were once believed to be a separate group of people, but later they joined the Cherokee. There was a boy in this clan who liked to leave home and live in the mountains. He would not eat at home but started off at first light of dawn to be gone all the day. Each day as he returned, his appearance changed with the growth of hair upon his back. Soon, the hair not only grew on his back, but also on his face, which was most unusual.

His mother and father became worried, as mothers and fathers should be worried about such an occurrence. They tried to talk with their son, but he would not speak. The mother and father spoke with others in their family. They tried to speak with the son, but he would not answer. The elders of this clan tried to talk with him, but again he would not respond. All that he had was hair to show; that was all that he had.

The other villages heard of this one. They sent over medicine men to speak with him or give him herbs. This son would not respond. He drank the herbs. He took the medicine. But he did not change. He did not speak; he was quiet. Others came to him. They followed him to the forest early in the morning. They returned at night. They, too, began to grow hair. Soon, they, too, did not speak.

The Ani-Tsa'guhi were concerned. They tried and tried to help these-with-the-hair. Soon these-with-the-hair did not return from the forest. Messengers were sent into the forest to find these-with-the-hair. The messengers returned, and they taught the Ani-Tsa'guhi this chant:

First Bear Chant

He-e! Ani-Tsa-guhi, Ani-Tsa'guhi, akwandu'li e'lanti ginun'ti;
He-e! Ani-Tsa-guhi, Ani-Tsa'guhi, akwandu'li e'lanti ginun'ti,
Yu!

[He-e! Ani-Tsa-guhi, Ani-Tsa'guhi, I want to lay them low on
the ground;
He-e! Ani-Tsa-guhi, Ani-Tsa'guhi, I want to lay them low on
the ground, Yu!]

Bear hunters would start each morning by fasting and would
not eat until near dusk. They would sing this song as they left the
camp in the morning, but they never would sing this chant twice
in the same day.

Second Bear Chant

This chant was for the bear hunter, for it called the bears to
come to a place where the hunter would be waiting:

He-e! Hayuya'haniwa', hayuya'haniwa', hayuya'haniwa',
hayuya'haniwa',
Tsistuyi'ne'handu'yanu',Tsistuyi'nehandu'yany'—Yoho-o!
He-e! Hayuya'haniwa', hayuya'haniwa',
hayuya'haniwa', hayuya'haniwa',
Kuwahi'i'ne'handu'yanu',Tsistuyi'nehandu'yany'—Yoho-o!
He-e! Hayuya'haniwa', hayuya'haniwa',
hayuya'haniwa', hayuya'haniwa',
Uyahyei'ne'handu'yanu',Tsistuyi'nehandu'yany'—Yoho-o!
He-e! Hayuya'haniwa', hayuya'haniwa', hayuya'haniwa',
hayuya'haniwa',
Gate'gwa'ne'handu'yanu', Tsistuyi'nehandu'yany' Yoho-o!
Ule-nu'aschi'tadeya'statakuhi'gun'nage astu'tsiki.

[He-e! Hayuya'haniwa', hayuya'haniwa', hayuya'haniwa',
hayuya'haniwa',
In Tsistu'yi you were conceived—Yoho!
He-e! Hayuya'haniwa', hayuya'haniwa', hayuya'haniwa',
hayuya'haniwa',

In Kuwa'hi you were conceived—Yoho!
　　He-e! Hayuya'haniwa', hayuya'haniwa', hayuya'haniwa',
hayuya'haniwa',
In Uya'hye you were conceived—Yoho!
　　He-e! Hayuya'haniwa', hayuya'haniwa', hayuya'haniwa',
hayuya'haniwa',
In Gate'gwa you were conceived—Yoho!]

10. Me'gis

The water of salt covered the earth. The old ones watched the water, waiting for a sign to come forth and guide them. Four years later, a large white shell rose out of the salt waters. It gave warmth to the people. It brought light to the people.

All at once it sank. There was no more light. There was no more warmth. The old ones waited. It rose to the surface and appeared again on the great river that drains the water of the Great Lakes. It brought warmth. It brought light.

All at once it sank. Death came to the wig'i'wams of the old ones, and they slowly began to die. The times were hard, cold, dark, and lonely. It rose again to the surface and reflected the rays of the sun at Bow-e-ting [Sault Ste. Marie]. It remained for a long time.

All at once it sank. It went down to the depths of Bow-e-ting and sank deep down to the dark world. Here it remained for a long time. For the last time the An-ish-in-aub-ag were left in darkness and misery.

Then it rose again once more. Its bright back shown at Mo-ning-wun-a-kaun-ing [La Pointe Island], where it has been since. It holds the light and wisdom that have guided people since that time. It reaches even the most remote village of the widespread Ojibwa. The shell is the emblem of the great Me'gis of the people.

Grandfather Paul smiled, and, using his hands, eyes, and the beat of his moccasined feet, chanted this story:

The Me'gis means the Me-da-we religion.
The old ones lived on the shores of the east.
They suffered the sickness and death.
The Great Spirit, with the help of Ma'ahbo'zho,

the great common uncle of An-is-in-aub-ag, granted the
people life, life restored, life prolonged.
The people, the old ones, moved from the shores
of the great water to the west.
The Me-da-we lodge was pulled down, and it was
not erected again until the Me'gis was seen again.
In the course of time, this town was deserted and the people
    continued west.
They would not light their fires until they reached the
shores of Lake Huron, where again
the rituals and ceremonies were performed.
Again these were forgotten, and the
Me-da-we lodge was taken down and
not built again until the people gathered at
Bow-e-ting, where it remained for many winters.
Still the Ojibwa moved west again,
and for a long time the Me-da-we lodge was
put back up on the island of La Pointe
and here the pale face appeared among them.

Now the ceremony is to be performed in its purest
and most original form.
    All the old ones lived for a full term of life granted to
them by the Great Spirit. The forms of many old people were
mingled with each oncoming generation. The many words have
been told to us over and over and over and over again by our
fathers for many years, births, deaths, and sunsets. This chant-
story helps us to remember the ways, struggles, and life of the
old ones.

11. Mide'wiwin of the Ojibwa

When people were ill, they were given a *Maski'kiwa'bu,* or medicine broth—the first liquid medical preparation. After this, they were given stronger teas from trees, plants, or grasses that had important mythic qualities as well as herbal healing power. One such plant was the *Zhingwak,* white pine, the needles of which were crushed and applied to relieve headaches.

Regardless of the disease or the cure, one of the most important steps of the medicine healer was the chant or song that went along with the herbal remedy. Each of the phrases was repeated before advancing to the next—one song occupying from fifteen minutes to two hours:

Ki-ne-ne-wi-in mani-i-do-ye-win.
Ki-zhik-ki-win-da-mun.
O-we-nen, hwin'?
Wi-dzhi-i-nan.
Nu-wa-ni-ma'na nin-guls'?
Ni-ee-ni.

Ni-nin-de, e,o,ya.
A-ni-na'-nesh-mi-I-an ni-na-wi-to.
Man-i-do-wi-an ni-me-shine-mi-an, shine-mi-an-do-mi.
We-gi-kwo Ke-mi-ni-nan.
Mi-shok kwot, dzhe-man-i-do-yan.
Wi-ka-ka-nun-e-nan.

[I rock you; you are that spirit.
The Sky I tell you.
Who is it, who?
The man helping me.

Have I told you the truth, my son?
Rest.

My heart, I am there in fullness of harmony.
I follow with my arms.
Knowledge comes from the heart; the heart reaches to sources
    of medicine in the earth.
The power comes from making clear sky (or clay, water, air).
The sky—if clear—holds good spirit.
Spirit fill the body with secrets of the earth.]

The Mide' have a chant that brings the blessing knowledge
of plants and other sacred objects taken from the ground. One
can learn it only by being a member of the Mide'wiwin people:

Na-witsh-tshi na-kum-ii-en a-na-pi-a?
We-nen-ne en'-da-yan.
Mo-ki-yan-na a-witsh-i-gum'-mi.
Wen-dzhi-ba-pi-a?
Zha-zha-bui-ki-bi-nan wig'e-wan.
Ya-ho-hon-ni-yo.
Ni-wo-we-ni-nan ki-bi-do-na.
Mide' ni-ka-nak kish-o-we-ni-mi-ko.
Ba-dzhi-ke-o gi-mand ma-bis-in-da-a.
Kwa-yak-in di-sha in-da-ya.
Kwe-tshi-ko-wa-ya ti-na-man.
O-wi-yo-in en-do-ma mak-kwin-en-do-o-ma.
O-wi-yo-in en-do-ma mak-kwin-en-do-o-ma.
Na-ni-ne kwe-we-an,an'.
He-wog, e',e'.

[When I am out of hearing, where am I?
In my house I can see.
When I rise it brings me new life, and I take it.
Spirit, why am I happy? I am happy. (pause)
The spirit says there is plenty of medicine in the Mide'
    wig'i'wam.
Sacred medicine is in the ground.

I come bringing this to you for you to have better health.
I have found favor in the eyes of my Mide' healers.
I hear the singer bring the spirit to speak to us.
I will go into the medicine lodge now that I am ready.
I am taking sacred objects and herbs to make me live.
I give you medicine and a lodge, also.
I give you medicine and a lodge, also.
The spirit has brought medicine from the sky to grow from
    the earth.
I have the medicine now in my body, in my heart.]

Vision Quests

Vision quests occur when people seek out where they are and what they need to feel whole. A person may pack up his four sticks of jerky, some water, some tools, a blanket, and go on a walk-about for four days. This is done only when there is another person to help.

The vision seeker and his follower arrange a meeting location on a mountain. The two walk separately, not within vision of each other. At night they can see each other's fire smoke, but in the day they are alone. If one is in need or is hurt, he can build a fire during the day, or wait until the fourth day. If he does not arrive at the agreed-upon meeting place, the other backtracks and locates the missing party. This is of utmost importance. There are mountain lions, wild coyotes that get desperate, and many rattlesnakes.

The vision quest promotes deep meditation. Many times a person will go to one location, staying for all four days. He will chant, sing, sleep and dream, walk close to camp, and let his "need" spirit leave and allow the "power" spirit to enter into him. Particular power spirits can be used such as the badger, mountain lion, bear, or snake. Also, there are the star spirits, sun and moon spirits, the wind, the Cloud People spirits, and more. The purpose of the vision quest is to let logic go and allow the soul to guide the inner self. This can be quite healing, though the need to follow real responsibilities and the truth of life is always there.

Smoke visions are used in the Southwest. Some people call them sweat baths, or "sweats." The smoke from an enclosed fire can make the patient sweat profusely and produce visions in the heart. Men go down into kivas deep in Old Earth Woman. They enter into Old Earth Woman and are held in her embrace. They build a fire and chant. Smoke from the fire rises through the air hole, and the prayers are carried to the men's spirit holder, Old Man Sky. Women build pit houses with wooden roofs of cedar poles wrapped in willow withes. These roofs lift skyward to Old Man Sky. The hot fires are doused with water, and the chants are taken deep into the Old Earth Woman. There is balance. Smokes or sweats, chants, or kiva prayers are rarely, if ever, done alone. The power of the group holds the power of the prayers.

Myth and ritual are grounded in visionary experience: the simple observations provide a foundation as the vision reveals the direction of power and guidance. For Native Americans, vision is as central to religious practice, ceremonial ritual, and literature as the myth born from it.

Visual power attests to the passage of life, to rites of passage. The ability to "receive" a vision is considered a mark of wisdom and maturity. Visions also are associated with rites of purification—including realizations of what is yet to be from what has happened. The vision quest brings about a metaphysical awareness of the real truth, namely, the sacred songs, religious ceremonies, treasured objects, and the responsibilities of everyday harmonious life. Sometimes details of the visions are within the seer; other times they are shared.

1. Tusayan Walpi

In the beginning all men lived together in the lowest depths in a region of darkness and moisture. Their bodies were deformed and horrible, and they suffered constantly in their pain, moaning and crying continually. Myu'ingwa, or the Spirit of the Feeling World, and the Baholikonga, a crested serpent of the water who brings vision, were called by the old men, and these two brought them a seed. The men put this seed into the moist, fertile world where they lived, and it yielded a magic growth of cane.

The cane grew up and up and up and up through the cracked roof. The people climbed up the cane to another world. It was dim, with little light, and there were some plants they could eat that helped them in their pain. Another seed fell, and they placed this in the damp, moist earth; and there grew another cane that the people could climb to a higher plane where the light was brighter and the plants produced even better food. Animals they had never seen before also lived there. Another seed fell to them, and they planted it.

It grew up and up and up and up, and they went up with it. This trip brought them to the pine tree, which they climbed to a surface. There they found twins singing and pulling people up and out of that world into *their* world. Some were not strong enough or wise enough or able enough to follow. The twins sang more songs, and others made it up, for they could see in the songs that they needed to move. Some should not have been allowed to come, but they came anyway.

Myu'ingwa sent through this place all the germs of all living life. This is why all kivas have pine ladders and a door always open to allow life to move up and down from the Old Earth Woman.

All the people who came up were collected, and different families were placed with different names. This was done by the twins, who were called Pekonghoya, the older, and Balinahoya, the younger—also referred to as Echo. They were helped by their grandmother Kohkyang wuhti, or Spider Woman. She told the people to live on the mountains or on the plains, to build lodges or lean-tos or shelters to keep them from the wind and rain. She and her grandsons gave each family gifts and told them that each had a message for a pathway that would help the families find their place on the Old Earth Woman.

The Hopituh (or Hano) were given the vision to build sweathouses, and they each took separate paths. They made migrations to various places, and the groups that moved to Tusayan at different times came from different directions. But they all were Snake People. The old one who remembers the vision quest that became a myth was from Nyumy. He tells of the migration:

At the time the people moved on their separate paths, they lived in snake skins. Each group or family had a separate snake-skin bag. They all hung their snake skins on the end of a rainbow, which they swung around and around and around and around until it touched the top of Navaho Mountain. The bags dropped from the rainbow and landed on the mountain where they were to build their homes. They arranged their snake-skin bags, emerged from them as men and women, and built their five-sided homes of stone.

The spirits sent a brilliant star that rose in the southeast sky and shone down for a long time before it disappeared. The old ones thought, "Beneath that star there must be more people." They moved toward the place where they had seen the star. They cut a cane, set it in the ground, and watched it until the star reappeared and shone at the base of the cane. Slowly the star illuminated the cane from base to top. Then the star disappeared.

The star reappeared, but not every night. There were times when it was quiet for many years and then would shine again. When it did not shine, the people built homes and waited. They waited until the star shone again, and when it touched the top of the sacred cane, the people moved. When our people reached Wipho, a few miles north of Walpi, the star disappeared and never was seen again. They built a house there, and after a time Masauwu [the spirit of the face of Old Earth Woman] came and told the people to move farther down the valley to the east and middle mesa, and there the people stayed and grew corn.

2. Mountain Way

The visions bring harmony, peace, substance, and subsistence to the one while helping all. A Zuni woman lived in a community where everyone was starving, greedy, and disloyal. It is said that the people used each other like pouring sand in an empty arroyo. There was no pride or respect.

The Zuni woman left her people. Her body was dirty and her clothes were rags, but her spirit was strong with hope. She walked for four days across the land until she came to a group of trees. Her hunger ate at her. Her feet ached. Her spirit held hope. She sat down with her back against a tree and rested, holding hope in her being. She let her head lean back against the strong pine tree trunk. Her eyes closed, letting sleep take her to another place, a place of visions.

The Bear people came. The Bear people brought her the healing. They sang:

People of the mountains and rocks,
I see you wish to be paid respect.
I give you corn pollen and hummingbird feathers,
and I send to you precious stones and tobacco,
which you must smoke.
It has been lighted by the sun's rays, and for this
I beg you to give me a good dance, be with me.
Earth, I beg you to give me a good dance, and
I offer to you food of hummingbirds' plumes and
precious stones and tobacco to smoke, lighted
by the sun's rays, to pay for using you for
the dance.
Make a good solid ground for me,
that the spirits who come to see the dance may be

pleased at the ground their people dance upon.
Make my people healthy and strong of mind
and body.

Visions of tied feathers, tobacco, and precious stones came
to the sleeping maiden. The stones were wrapped in leather and
hung from a hand-held stick. Carved dry gourds were rattled by
spirits that danced around this sleeping maiden.

From below [the earth] corn comes;
I walk with you.
From above [as water] the young come;
I walk with you.
From above the plants that grow [come to the earth];
I walk with you.
From below [the earth] corn pollen comes;
I walk with you.

Birds of all colors flew overhead in her vision, and from their
mouths fell seeds of all colors. The seeds fell down, down, down,
down, and the earth opened and swallowed them up. Plants
grew, entwined, and rose up in their splendor to the sky. Buds
swelled, opened, flowered, and matured into fine fat corn, beans,
and squash.

The wind blew, and the Zuni woman opened her eyes. She
reached out her hand and touched the plants that grew around
her. She gathered up one corn, bean, squash and walked back to
her village. The people ran to her, each one trying to grab the
food she held.

She taught the people the lesson of her vision. Now, the
earth shakes with the dancers, the fields are fertile with food, and
the sky still holds vision ripe with hope.

May your path always be of beauty.
May pollen always be on your feet.

3. Black Turtle Chant

Visions are reconstructed as closely as possible from the metaphysical to the material plane. The re-enacting of the vision is done so that the power can be revealed and appreciated. Re-enactment is a normal procedure for a vision of this chant type. The vision relates the direct rules for the dance itself, the behavior of the dancers, the articles they need, and the social etiquette. This vision was revealed so that it could be renewed here on earth to show respect to the spirits:

The Black Turtle now approaches, wearing and shaking his belt of black night;
The Black Turtle now approaches, wearing and shaking his belt of black night.

Understand, my brothers, it is the sun that gives me the magic I need;
Understand, my brothers, it is the sun that brings a trance vision to me,
As I walk, wearing and shaking my belt of black night,
As I walk, wearing and shaking my belt of black night.

Turtle, turtle, where is the pond that you swim in?
Turtle, turtle, where is the water that you live within?
Turtle, turtle, where is the pond that you live in, wearing and shaking your belt of black night?
The Black Turtle now approaches, wearing and shaking his belt of black night;
The Black Turtle now approaches, wearing and shaking his belt of black night.

In the morning, we sing many songs;
At mid-day we sing many songs;
In the evening, I join in the singing, too.

The images found in the visions are not symbolic in the usual sense; that is, the animal in the vision or chant does not stand for something else, but for itself. The symbol is perceived as it truly is—a frog or turtle or mountain—yet it holds a metaphysical concept as well. This takes the symbol to a sacred meaning, in that everything on this earth is sacred. All of life is sacred. Visions, then, are perceived in a very sacred manner with great respect.

Those who learned from the Frog became known as Frog People (Tak-yainna-kwe). Their visions enabled them to understand Frog. Those who loved the plants of the earth became known as the Seed People (Taatem'hlanah-kwe). Those who planted and held the knowledge of grass were known as Petaa-kwe. Those of the Tobacco were known as Ana-kwe. Those who loved the earth fire became known as Badger People (Tonashi-kwe). They knew of the gifts from the earth, and they were chosen for their totems, which came from visions.

The People of the North took on the knowledge of the Bear People (Ainshi-kwe), Coyote People (Suski-kwe), or Deer People (Shohoita-kwe) the Crane People (Ka'lokta'kwe), and so on.

These groups of Summer People and Winter People were then divided into clans or kin ties. The strongest of these people were to become the Wise Ones, who were equal to priests. Shiwana-kwe were the High Wise Ones; and the Newe-kwe were the Medicine Holders, who knew of healing, poisons, and evil ways. Their great father was Paiyatuma, the Spirit of the Dew and the Dawn.

4. Paiyatuma's First Commandments

This chant is sung to bring about a vision:

Itamumi Kuyivawicha;
Itamumi umuh kuyap, kuyi wutay'a,
Iyo, iyo!
Iyo, iyo!

[Raise the water jars;
Pour the water on us,
Cold, cold!
Cold, cold!]

Paiyatuma was the holder of the commandments of the First People. Paiyatuma taught the Newe-kwe how to fertilize the virgin plants, animals, and maidens. The seed-priests became the holders of the sacred substances used in medicinal healing. Shiwana-kwe taught the people how to plume the feathers of birds and make them into clouds to bring rain with prayers. The coming of rain brought the Cloud People, who had the power to heal the sick.

Another vision chant was then sung:

Hevebe Tawi
Nana hopipagi
qoyungwunuka kuyiva;

Nanu hopipago
Sikiangwunuka
kuyiva;

Angu'u,
huwan,
Hawiwokialyata.

[Now from the east
the white dawn
has risen;

Now from the east
the yellow dawn
has risen;

Notice,
awaken,
look on us with our respect.]

During the preparation time for the rain ceremony, the Seed People came and sat in a circle telling their stories. They were blessed by the Newe-kwe. For eight days there was a fasting, and on the eighth day the mothers and fathers brought their children to the plains where the grasses grew. There they danced and prepared the sacred medicine seeds. All night they danced back and forth, back and forth, back and forth. They moved their hands from side to side, then motioned with their prayer wands up and down to show the growth of the plants.

The keepers of the great shells, Badger Clan, would then come into the circle and walk to the center fire and throw the shells in. The seed keepers would then throw their seed into the fire. The substance of all life comes from the water of life, shells, and the growth of life—seeds. The Badger Clan would keep the fire going, which represented the heat of the sun and the warmth of the earth—all vital to life, all vital to good health, all vital to perpetuation.

5. Noko'mis of the Menomini

At the time of the first people, there was a woman called Noko'mis. She gave birth to a living child in soft, dry grass. She lay nursing this infant on the ground near her wig'i'wam. Four days prior to giving birth to her own child, Noko'mis's daughter and granddaughter died. She placed her newborn infant under a wooden bowl to protect it while she went to wash the dead ones. She washed, then took the bodies of her dead daughter and grandchild and buried them away from her wig'i'wam. When she returned to her wig'i'wam four days later, she sat down and mourned. At the end of the fourth day, she heard a noise. When she looked she found the wooden bowl was moving. She lifted it and found her child. The child was a white rabbit with quivering ears. She was very pleased to find it and said, "Oh, little rabbit, my Ma'nabush!"

She cared for the little rabbit and nurtured it. One day the rabbit sat up on its haunches and slowly hopped across the floor of the wig'i'wam. Each time it jumped, the floor shook. Each time it jumped the earth shook. The *ana'maqki-u,* the evil ones who chose to live underground, were frightened. They called to each other, "A *ma'nido* has been born and we must destroy it!"

They started to think of ways to kill Ma'nabush. But Ma'nabush grew and grew out of a rabbit and became a young man. He asked his old mother, whom he called Grandmother, for some help: "Old one, make me four sticks, that I may sing."

She cut the wood, carved for him four sticks, and he hit them together to make music. He sang, "I shall make more animals; I shall make more people; I can create a fire that will reach the sky; I can carve an arrow that will bring food to those who are here."

When the people were made, he told them of his sticks and called them *Mita'wit,* or curing sticks. He gave them medicine bags made out of mink skins, weasel skins, black rattlesnake skins, and panther skins.

Here, then, is another story of Ma'nabush and his medicine:

Ma'nabush, the Great One, found that his brother had been killed. He mourned for him, and on the fifth day of his sorrow, Ma'nabush found that he was not alone. Walking behind him was his brother. Ma'nabush thought this very strange. He walked around his brother and poked him. It was his brother, the brother who had died.

"How can you be alive if you were killed?" Ma'nabush asked his brother.

His brother told him, "Our people will die, but if we mourn their loss and remember what was good about them, they will return again."

Ma'nabush studied his brother and saw that his body was growing longer and longer as the sun got closer to the western horizon.

"You are but a shadow vision," he said. "You are not a real brother." His brother did not speak again. Ma'nabush said, "You return to the place of the setting sun. You will have the name Na'qpote, and you will have to take care of all those others who die and go to the same place."

Ma'nabush walked along the land until he came to the river. There lived Mi'sikine'bik, the great fish. The great fish told Ma'nabush that if any people came near the water he would eat them. Ma'nabush cut down some birch trees and made a canoe. He had a plan of attack for the great fish.

The great fish noticed him and swallowed him and the canoe. Ma'nabush found others in the stomach of the great fish. He asked Buffalo, "What are you doing in here, my uncle? How did you find your way into the belly of the great fish?"

Buffalo spoke sadly, "I was eating the fresh green grass that grows by the river, and this great fish leaped out of the water and swallowed me. Now I am alone and miss my people."

Ma'nabush asked the others, and they had similar stories. Many of the animals were sick. Ma'nabush gathered them together and showed them how to dance in ceremony. They gathered in two lines and danced up and down. This made the great fish angry. They continued to dance, and the great fish became sick and threw them up out of his belly onto the land.

The animals were very glad to be free, but many had been inside the great fish a long time and were sick. Ma'nabush walked to the high mountain of the rising sun. He called out to the large white bear, Owa'sse. When Owa'sse came down from the mountain, Ma'nabush drew an arrow and shot through the body of Owa'sse. Ma'nabush killed Owa'sse. The blood of Owa'sse ran down the mountainside and stained it so that all could find the place. That is where the people get the medicine used by the medicine men and the animals.

Ma'nabush felt very strong after this good adventure. He walked into a village and told the people that there was nothing he could not do. He was strong, wise, and magical, and no one could defeat him. Ma'nabush bragged to all he met. This was not good.

A young mother heard him bragging and took him aside. "If you are so strong and wise," she said, "then I have a challenge for you. You come home with me and get someone whom I love and care for to do as you say. Then perhaps I will believe that you are capable of what you say. Otherwise, I question you."

Ma'nabush stepped back. "You want me to come home with you for a testing?" he asked. People had gathered around them.

"Yes," she answered, "but I will not be alone with you. The one who tests will be there, and this one is very strong."

Ma'nabush followed the young mother home. There on soft blankets lay a small, young baby. The child was cooing and rolling around on the blanket. Ma'nabush knelt down on the floor next to the baby. The baby studied Ma'nabush. Ma'nabush spoke to the baby, and the baby started to cry. Ma'nabush made funny faces and funny noises, and the baby stopped crying and smiled. Ma'nabush sat back and spoke to the baby about his adventures and about his own bravery. Now and then the baby rolled around and smiled.

Ma'nabush said to the baby, "Get up. Let us go for a walk. Get up." The baby continued to roll around on the blanket.

Ma'nabush sat back and spoke firmly: "Get up, and let us go for a walk. Come, get up." The baby just looked at him.

Ma'nabush spoke harshly: "Get up, and let us go for a walk. Get up!" The baby burst into tears and wailed and cried.

Ma'nabush said, "Stop that. Let us go for a walk!" The baby continued to cry.

Ma'nabush got up and spoke to the young mother. "You were right," he said. "I am not as powerful as I thought."

6. Earth Magician Vision

In one particular ceremony, the Apache shaman helped cure certain diseases with special pollens. The healer sang and prayed to the powers that might inform him of the illness and how to proceed with the cure. The ceremony was repeated on four consecutive nights: it began at dark and continued until midnight, when everyone dined on food provided by the patient's relatives. At the conclusion of the fourth night, the healer sucked out poison supposedly planted in the patient by an evil shaman or witch and spat it into a fire. The shaman would then impose restrictions on the patient, often dietary, such as a prohibition against eating liver. The healer might also give a protective charm to the supplicant.

Every Apache band but the Kiowa celebrated the Mountain Spirits, originally part of the religion practiced by the Pueblo, another Southwestern people. The Mountain Spirits generally represented good power and could protect people from illness. They were invoked in a healing ceremony similar to the one just described, except that it used masked dancers.

As with the Apache ceremony, the patient approached the shaman and formally presented his or her case, lavishing gifts on the healer and marking him with pollen. In short, the patient sought the shaman's pity, the emotion that led the healer to salve the wound.

If the shaman accepted the case, he selected four men to act as masked dancers and then painted them in an elaborate style. Meanwhile, the patient's relatives built a corral with a fire burning in the center. The corral had openings to each direction. The patient was then placed in the corral to await the dancers. Drums sounded as the dancers approached from the east, trailing the shaman, who sang and danced as the troupe entered. He stepped toward the flame, circled it clockwise, and then retraced his steps toward the east.

The four dancers circled the fire four times, assumed positions of worship, and followed the shaman to the ailing supplicant, who daubed them with paint. Next, the shaman approached the patient, asked where he hurt, and then directed the dancers to execute a series of steps four times. After the last series, the lead dancer ceremonially exhaled in every direction to blow the illness away. The other dancers did likewise, then left the corral.

This ceremony was repeated, with slight variations, for three more nights. On the second or third night, the healer might check the patient's progress. He pressed abalone—a mollusk with a spiral shell—against the patient's forehead. If the abalone stuck, his chances of recovery were good. If not, he faced prolonged illness. In either case, the ceremony continued for the full four nights.

After a favorable prognosis, the shaman prescribed remedies. He might instruct the patient to avoid certain foods. He also warned the patient that if he violated these restrictions, disease would recur. If the outlook seemed bad, the shaman prayed for the afflicted person until he recovered. Sometimes this ceremony was performed on a larger scale to benefit the whole community.

Just as the Apache believed in the life-force, they also believed that death held mysterious powers. When someone died, his or her relatives began a period of mourning. They wailed, cut their hair, and donned old clothing. Older relatives then prepared the corpse for burial. Some Apache were afraid to touch dead bodies and enlisted strangers or captives to lay them to rest. Others enacted a burial ritual that could have originated no earlier than the mid-16th century when the Spaniards introduced horses to the Apache.

Also in Apache mythology, when someone died, his or her body released a spirit that was guided into the underworld by the ghosts of dead relatives. The Lipan, Jicarilla, and Western Apache all believed the underworld consisted of two sections. One was a pleasant, green place inhabited by the ghosts of virtuous people. The other was a barren place inhabited by ghosts, witches, and magicians. Apache and Pima both share in this song, which, even though the languages differ, expresses the same concept:

Earth Magician Vision

Earth Magician shapes this world;
Behold what he can do!
Round and smooth he molds it;
Behold what he can do!

Earth Magician makes the mountains;
Listen to what he has to say!
Earth Magician makes the mesas;
Listen to what he has to say!

Earth Magician shapes this world;
Earth Magician makes its mountains;
Makes all larger, larger, larger;
Into the earth the Magician glances;
Into its mountain depths he can see.

Earth Healer makes Grey Spider's web;
Grey Spider spins a web from earth to sky;
Earth Healer throws ice for the sun and moon,
Throws ice water for stars in the sky!

I have made the sun! cries Earth Healer.
I have made the sun!
Throwing it high,
Throwing it north, west, south, and east
To run the course of its path.

I have made the moon! cries Earth Healer.
I have made the moon!
Throwing it high,
throwing it north, west, south, and east
To run the course of its path.

I have made the stars! cries Earth Healer.
I have made the stars!
High above the earth, I threw them;
All sacred objects above the earth, I have made them.
And now I order them to glisten with life!

7. Cherokee Healing

The sweat bath, common among almost all the tribes north of Mexico, except for the central and eastern Eskimo, was thought of as a cure-all in sickness. The tribes appeared to have a great regard for this ceremonial observance. The Cherokee frequently used sweat baths, bleeding, rubbing, and cold baths for healing, and their ceremonies featured beads and other paraphernalia. They looked upon the sweat bath as a medical application, which was used with the plunge bath. The heat of the former mixed with cold of the latter brought about many visions.

The patient who wished cleansing through the sweat bath was put into the *a'si* (a small, earth-covered log house only high enough to allow one to sit). The patient would undress and place large, hot boulders near his chosen place in the log house. Then a concoction of beaten parsnip roots would be poured over the boulders. The door was closed so that no air could enter from the outside, and the patient remained in the sweltering steam. Many times the sweat itself would bring apparitions to the patient and guide him on his path to healing. Generally, patients plunged into cold water before leaving the ceremony.

Bleeding also was used, for example to heal rheumatism. There were two methods. In one, a small cupping horn was applied after scarification by a flint or a piece of broken glass. Blood was drawn out, and with it would come the cause of the pain, such as a splinter or a small pebble. The healer then would cover this wound with a mud-healing pack.

In the second case, simple scratching was used to encourage the bleeding. This painful method usually involved a brier or a rough flint arrowhead, but for some illnesses the scratching was done with a rattlesnake's tooth or the rough surface of a turkey bone. The loss of blood along with the painful procedure itself could induce visions.

The scratches were not cut so deeply as to cause serious injury, yet the blood would flow enough for the medicine to work. This also was done on players or foot racers to toughen up their muscles. Medicine was rubbed into the wounds as they bled, and then the patient was carried to the river and plunged in cold water. The scratches were washed using a switch, which kept the blood from clotting. For rheumatism and other local diseases, the scratching was confined to that part of the body affected.

Rubbing was used for pains and swellings of the abdomen. Done with the tip of the finger or the palm of the hand, it should not be confused with massage. In one of the Gahuni formulas for treating snake bites, the healer told the patient to rub in a direction contrary to that in which the snake coils, because this would uncoil the poison.

Blowing was used on the head, hands, and other parts of the body, an important part of the ceremonial healing. In some ceremonies, healers blew on the right hand, the left foot, the left hand, and the right foot, making the sign of harmony or the cross. To heal, the patient combined the sensation of the blowing and the mental picture of evil leaving the body.

Bathing in a river was called "going to water." It was done on many occasions such as at each new moon, before eating new food, prior to a dance, and after playing a game. Or it could accompany praying for a long life, removing evil spells, or treating many diseases.

The chant for bathing was as follows:

Sge' Ha-nag'wa usinuli'yu hatu'gani'ga Hige 'yagu'ga tsuwa'tsi'la gi'gage tsiye'la skina'du-lani'ga. O O digwada'ita. Sa'ka'ni tugwadune'luhi. Atsanu'gi gi gage skwasu'hisa'tani'ga. Kulsta'lagi kulsta'lagi kulsta'lagi sak'ka'ni nu'tatanu'ta. Ditu nu na gi dagwu'lasku gwu deganu'y tsai'ga. Gala'nu tse ta'gwu dagwadnune'lidise'sti. Sge!

[Listen, you have drawn near to hear the words. You have been born from the foam where you are moving about as one. You have placed your fluid into me and put it upon my body. It is red. My name is Gatigwanasti. The blue has come upon me. You have come and clothed me with a red dress. She is of the deer clan. She has become blue. You have directed her path straight to where I have my feet, and I shall feel full of you. Listen!]

Now it is time for the stories.

8. Ahsonnutli

The first three worlds were not good. The first three worlds were not healthy. The first three worlds kept the People moving. The first three worlds made the People lightheaded and dizzy. The first three worlds were of darkness, and the People said there must be light.

In Ute Mountain there lived two women. One was called Ahsonnutli. She was the turquoise hermaphrodite. The second was called Yolaikaiason, or White Shell Woman. These two women were called upon by the Navaho. The People told them that they needed light.

The Navaho had already separated light into several colors. Next to the floor was the color white that indicated the coming of the dawn. On top of the white was blue that was spread for the morning, and on the blue was yellow that symbolized the sunset. The next color was black, representing the night.

The Navaho people had prayed long and hard for the coming of the light, but nothing had happened. There still was not light. They continued to pray. Ahsonnutli and Yolaikaiason arrived and told them to keep praying, and if their prayers were pure and good they would be answered. The People prayed:

Night Spirit, Night Spirit, rise up and call out for us.
Night Spirit, Night Spirit, rise up and listen for the coming of
    the colors.

Night Spirit carried his ear with him. Night Spirit rose up and with his ear he listened. Night Wind called out, "There is a young person at the falls." Night Spirit called to his messenger, Shooting Star. Shooting Star went to the young person at the falls and brought him to Night Spirit.

Night Spirit said, "Ahsonnutli is the *ahst-jeo'hltoi* [hermaphrodite]. She has white beads on her right breast and turquoise on her left breast. Go and pray to her and ask her to lay these sacred beads on the darkness of the night and sing your prayers. Sing your prayers with the love of her; sing your prayers with the love of light; sing your prayers of respect to her; sing your prayers of respect for her."

The young person from the falls went to Ahsonnutli. The young person from the falls spoke to Ahsonnutli: "You have carried the sacred white-shell beads, and you have carried the sacred turquoise beads for a long time. You should know what to say to the Night Spirit."

Ahsonnutli took a sacred crystal dipped in pollen. She marked eyes and a mouth on the turquoise. She marked eyes and a mouth on the white-shell bead. She formed a circle around these with the crystal, and she produced a slight light from the white shell bead and a greater light from the turquoise bead. The light was not enough.

Twelve men stood. Twelve men stood at each of the cardinal points. Forty-eight of the men were called to be at the crystal circle. After their arrival Ahsonnutli sang a song. The men sat down opposite her. They sat with great respect. The men joined in the song with her. The light did not change. The light was still not enough.

Two eagle plumes were placed upon each cheek of the turquoise. Two eagle plumes were placed upon each cheek of the white-shell beads. Two eagle plumes were placed at each of the cardinal points. The twelve men of the east placed twelve turquoise pieces at the east. The twelve men of the south placed twelve white-shell beads at the south. The twelve men of the west placed twelve turquoise pieces at the west, and those of the north placed twelve white-shell beads at that point.

Each one of the men dipped the crystal into corn pollen that had been blessed by Sun. They took the crystal and made a circle embracing the whole of the beads and the plumes. The wish still remained with no results. Ahsonnutli held the crystal over the turquoise face. It ignited into a blaze of light.

The People ran back, afraid of the great light. The intense heat increased. The men found the four points of heat so strong that they arose, but they could hardly stand as the Night Spirit was so close to them. They looked away from the bright light and saw two rainbows—one from east to west and the second from north to south. The heads and feet of the rainbows almost touched the tops of the men's heads. The men tried to raise the great light, but each time they got near it, they became afraid and could not do so.

Finally, a man and woman appeared. The men had never seen these two before and knew nothing of them. The man's name was Atseatsine, and the woman's name as At'seatsan. The men looked down out of respect, and with a voice in unison they asked the two, "Where can we find the sun?"

The two replied, "We know. The People down here are trying to raise it, and we heard your prayers. This is why we came."

"Chanteen [Sun's Rays]," called out the man. "I have the Chanteen. I have the crystal from which I can light the Chanteen. I have the rainbow. These three with my chant will rise up and bring the sun."

The People said, "Go and raise it. We respect you. We shall be courteous to you."

The man elevated the sun a short distance. The sun was heavy and it tipped. The plants and the grasses burned from the heat. The People were burned. The sun was still too close.

The People said to Atseatsine and At'seatsan, "Raise the sun higher, for it is too close. Lift it as high as the sun can rise."

Atseatsine and At'seatsan made four poles—two of turquoise and two of white-shell beads—and each was placed under the sun. These poles were raised by the twelve men at each of the cardinal points, high into the air. They could not get it high enough to prevent the People and the grasses from burning. The People then said, "Let us stretch the world."

The twelve men at each point pulled and stretched on the world. The sun rose as the world expanded, and it began to shine with less strength. When it reached the highest point, the heat became great and the People burned. They crawled everywhere, anywhere they could to find shade.

Then the voice of Darkness went four times around the world. The voice of Darkness went four times around the world, telling the men at the cardinal points to keep stretching the world. "Darkness is talking to you. Darkness is telling you that all this trouble will stop. The People are suffering; the People are burning; the darkness is strong; you must keep stretching, stretching, stretching, stretching."

The men blew and stretched. After a time, they saw the sun rise beautifully. The sun reached the meridian, and it was hot—but only hot, not burning. It was then just as it should be. The men looked out. The People looked out, and they could see that the earth was encircled first with the white dawn of day. The blue of early morning reached down and touched the earth, and all things were as they should be. Ahsonnutli told the twelve men to go to the east, south, west, and north, to hold up the sky and keep it strong. This brought about the Yiyanitsinni, the holders of the sky. They perform this task every day and for every day yet to come.

9. Hasjelti and Hostjoghon

Navaho Hasjelti and Hostjoghon were the children of Ah-sonnutli of the turquoise and Yolaikaiason, or White Shell Woman, also the wife of the sun. Ahsonnutli placed a pure ear of white corn down on the ground. Yolaikaiason placed an ear of yellow corn on the mountain where the fog meets the earth. The corn touched. The corn had union one with the other. The corn conceived.

The white corn gave birth to Hasjelti, and the yellow corn to Hostjoghon. These two became strong and fine. These two became whole and wise. These two became the songmakers of the world. The songmakers bring health to the singers. The songmakers bring wholeness to the lost. The songmakers hold harmony within their words.

The songmakers gave to the mountain of their birth (Henry Mountain in Utah) two songs and two prayers. They dressed the mountain in clothing of white-shell beads that held two eagle plumes placed on the head. This was good.

They then went to the Sierra Blanca mountains of Colorado. There they made two songs, two prayers, and dressed the mountain in clothing of white-shell beads with two eagle plumes placed upright upon the head.

The two then moved to San Mateo Mountain of New Mexico. Here they gave the mountain two songs, two prayers, and dressed this mountain in turquoise. They dressed this mountain in turquoise leggings and moccasins, and then they placed two eagle plumes on the head of the mountain.

Then they moved to San Francisco Mountain in Arizona. Here they made two songs and two prayers and dressed the mountain in abalone shells with two eagle plumes upon the head.

They next visited Ute Mountain and gave it two songs and two prayers and dressed it in black beads. This mountain also had two eagle plumes on its head. They then decided to return to the mountain of their birth and chose to meditate with song. They called to their mothers:

Mothers, we are only two.
Mothers, we are only two.
Mothers, there are many who need song.
Mothers, there need to be more of us.
Mothers, we are only two.
Mothers, let our numbers be increased.
Mothers, let our numbers grow.

The women placed more yellow corn on the mountain. The women placed more white corn on the mountain. The corn grew. The corn touched. The corn had union. The corn conceived. More were born on the mountain, enough born to place the two brothers on each of the four mountains. To these spirits of the mountains, the clouds came first. The brothers consulted together concerning what they should live upon, and they decided to make a game. This brought about the testings, the trials, and the games.

Navaho prayers for rain and snow are addressed to Hasjelti and Hostjoghon. These spirits stand on the mountain tops and call to the clouds to gather them. Hasjelti is the mediator between the Navaho and Sun. He prays in his glory to Sun:

Sun, give me the light of your being.
Sun, give me the wisdom of your mind.
Sun, give me the strength of your loins.
Sun, give me your arm so that I will be whole.
Sun, give me your rays so that the corn will grow.
Sun, give me your warmth so that the world will be fertile.

Hasjelti is called by the People using the great feathers. The choicest feathers and plumes are placed in the sacred smokes and attached to the prayer sticks offered to him.

From these great offerings, from these great feathers, came about the floating logs.

There was a man who thought on his life and the world around him. He wanted to sing a sacred song to these two strong spirits; but his songs were too short, and he felt that they were not being heard. Hasjelti appeared before him and said, "I can give to you more songs. I shall lead you."

The man nodded and spoke, "I will follow you, for this shall answer my prayers."

They went to a certain point in a box canyon in the Big Colorado River. There they called out and prayed for the four great spirits. The Hostjobokon came down and immediately began hewing logs of cottonwood.

Hasjelti said, "This will not do. Cottonwood becomes water-soaked and will sink. You must use pine."

The Hostjobokon then began boring the pine with flint. Hasjelti said, "This is slow work." Hasjelti then sang a sacred song, and a whirlwind hollowed out the pine logs.

The song-hunter entered the hollow log. Hasjelti closed the end with a cloud. The water of the river could not enter when the logs were launched upon the great waters. The Hostjobokon, accompanied by their wives, rode on the logs, and a couple rode on the end of each of the logs.

Hasjelti and Hostjoghon and two Naaskiddi walked on the banks to keep the logs from coming ashore. Hasjelti carried a squirrel skin filled with sacred tobacco. This was used to supply the great spirits on their journey. Hostjoghon carried a cane that—with eagle and turkey plumes and a gaming ring—was tied with two hummingbirds wrapped with a cotton cord.

The two Naaskiddi carried canes of lightning. These guided the great spirits on their way.

The logs floated a long distance down the river, and then they came to waters with a shore on one side only. Here they decided to land. They found people much like themselves. These people sang the song of the song-hunter's wish. They gave to the song-hunter many songs. They gave to the song-hunter painted pictures on a cotton blanket. They gave to him a meaning: "These pictures must go with the songs. If we give this blanket to you,

you will lose it. We will give you white earth and black coals that you will grind together to make black paint. We will give you white sand. We will give you yellow sand. We will give to you red sand. We will give to you the blue paint, and you will take white sand and black coals with a little bit of red and yellow sand. These together will give you blue."

The song-hunter stayed with the people until the corn was ripe. There he learned to eat corn, and he took some corn with him to the Navaho, who had never seen corn before. He showed them how to raise corn and how to eat it.

The logs would not go upstream. The logs would not move against the flow of the water. The song-hunter called to Sun. Sun sent down four sunbeams, and one was attached to each end of the logs. The song-hunter now arrived at the box canyon, where he emerged. There he separated the logs, placing an end of the solid log into the hollow end of the other, and planting this great pole in the river. It is there now.

The song that heals is the song of the old priest known as the song-hunter. His song is the song of the world.

10. Naiyenesgony and Tobaidischinni

The birth of saviors is told in many different Indian cultures. Naiyenesgony and Tobaidischinni were born from others' knowledge of the spirit world. The Navaho believe that the world was destroyed five times—the first time by a whirlwind; the second by huge hail stones; the third by a horrible disease known as "the spots" (one spot covered an entire face); and the fourth time by the inability to breathe, an episode known as the "time of coughing." The fifth time Naiyenesgony and Tobaidischinni traveled over the whole of the earth and slew all the evil spirits and monsters trying to destroy the earth.

Two boys were born at Tohatkle. Tohatkle is the place where the two rivers come together near Ute Mountain in Utah. They were conceived and born of Ahsonnutli and Yolaikaiason. Ahsonnutli had a very sacred beard under her right arm. Yolaikaiason carried a small ball of human skin under her left arm. This is what she used to make shells. When the shells were put under the chins of the boys, they became brilliant. The boys could then look out and see all things everywhere. This gaze was all right for a short time, but if they looked too long, their eyes became tired.

A black stick was placed on the forehead of Naiyenesgony. A blue stick was placed on the forehead of Tobaidischinni. When Naiyenesgony shook his head, the stick stayed on his forehead. He also felt something growing in the palm of his hand. When he looked at his palm, he found three kinds of seeds. He said to the People, "We must learn from this. We must plant these. We must learn from this."

Tobaidischinni shook his head, and the stick dropped off his forehead. He thought for a long, long time. He reached down and studied what it was that the stick had become. Tobaidischinni lifted up the changed-shape stick and said, "We must go by this. We must learn from this. These are points that hold power. We must go by this."

He picked up the deer horns, and when he did so, he learned why the deer shed their horns. Breath of healing came from the sticks, which were made to represent the originals. The sticks also were used to hold wounds and to heal wounds.

Tobaidischinni and Naiyenesgony grew fast. In four days they were as tall and strong as any man. On the fifth day they helped the people, and food was brought to those who held hunger. On the seventh day, the two young men went out in search of their father. Ahsonnutli did not tell them that she was their mother. She *did* tell them that as their mother lay in beams of Sun, he entered into her and they were conceived. The two young men then set out in search of their father. They asked her where their father might live, and she said that he had ceased to be.

The two young men did not believe this, and they set out in search of their father. They traveled to the east and came to the house of Sun. They asked the wife of Sun, Yol-aika-iason, if their father was home. She was shocked and told them to wait. The day ended, and as the Sun moved under the earth, he came to his home. There he found the two young men.

"What are these two doing here?" he asked his wife.

She replied, "You tell me that you never do anything that would hurt anyone. Yet you have two sons who have come in search of you, and I knew nothing of them. How could this have happened?"

Sun's face reddened with anger. "These are not my sons!"

Yol-aika-iason shook her head. "Look at them. Look at how strong they are. Look at the power within them, and you will see that they are your sons!"

Sun told the two young men to stand off in the distance. He wanted to prove to his good woman that these were not his sons. He threw a great roll of black clouds down on them. The weight and water of the clouds would kill the young men. The two stood watching the great roll of black clouds. They felt the moisture all around them. They felt the pressure of the clouds descending upon them. But the young men chanted the songs that they had been taught. The great roll of black clouds subsided and disappeared. The two young men were unhurt.

Sun called the two young men to him. He told them that they were to turn their backs to him. He took a sharp flint knife and pulled them back onto it. The knife was sharpened to glisten with the light of Sun. But the two young men were unhurt.

Sun stood back amazed. He nodded to his woman, Yol-aika-iason, and said, "You are a wise woman. You see more than I do. You are right; these are my sons. I do not know how this came to be, but they are my sons."

Yol-aika-iason smiled, for she was proud to know that these strong young men of great courage, wisdom, and ability were the offspring of Sun. Sun called his helpers Hasjelti and Toneennili to build a great sweat house and put the two young men in it. Hasjelti and Toneennili built the sweat house so that the heat would surely kill anyone who stayed in it for any time at all. Sun admired their work and approved of this, for he did not want the reputation of a father who did not know his own children.

Toneennili made a dark hole inside the sweat house. He told the young men to sit there, there in that hole. The young men did this. Toneennili then placed a large lava rock over the hole and built a fire over the rock. The rock became very hot. Sun ordered Toneennili to sprinkle sacred water on it four times and each time to sing the song of purity. Toneennili did this while the entrance to the sweat house was tightly sealed. After a time, Sun called to the young men, asking them to come out and see him. Toneennili and Hasjelti shook their heads. They knew that no one could live through such heat.

The rock moved. The rock moved away from the hole. The two young men stood up in the sealed sweat house and shook off the dirt. The two young men cut the sweat-house skins that sealed it and stepped out to meet Sun.

"We are here," they said to their father.

Yol-aika-iason spoke to Sun. "These are your sons. You need to accept them and learn from their wisdom."

Sun said, "You are my own. I have tried to destroy you. What is it that you want from me as your father?"

The two young men asked that they return to the woman whom they believed was their aunt.

Sun asked them again, "What is it that you wish from me as your father?"

They answered, "We want arrows that fly straight. We want bows that are light but can shoot with great weight. We need knives that know how to hit their mark. We need leggings that will keep our legs strong and firm. There are giants and meat eaters that are killing our people, and they need to die. There are tiny meat-eaters that suck the blood of our people, and they need to die. These we need to kill with lightning."

Sun gave the young men clothing that would protect them from harm. Sun gave them lightning that would kill the enemies. Sun gave them a great stone knife. This was good. This was as it should be. They left their father and Yol-aika-iason.

Naiyenesgony killed the evil ones with the lightning. Tobaidischinni scalped the evil ones with his knife. After all the enemies had been destroyed, Naiyenesgony and Tobaidischinni told the Navaho people, "Now we leave you. We must return to our home in the Ute Mountains. We will go to the place where the waters join in union. Before we leave we will give you ten songs and ten prayers that will bring good health and wisdom for your people."

Tobaidischinni became the parent of all the waters of this world. Then came the brothers.

11. Wind Mountain Brothers

The Tolchini lived at Wind Mountain. They were brothers, one to the other. One brother would leave the group and go out alone. He always returned with a gift. He would bring back a pine bough or corn, and each item had a story to go with it. The brothers thought that he was not of sound mind, and they would make fun of him and laugh at him. Yet, they were jealous, for he did have fine gifts and did tell fine stories.

They decided that they would test him. The Tolchini took their brother away from Wind Mountain to the rocky foothills of eastern San Mateo Mountain. There was nothing to eat except seed grass. The oldest of the brothers said, "Let us go out and hunt for some food." They told the brother, who always had gifts and stories, to stay at the camp.

After five days the brothers did not return. The gift-giver storyteller brother went out in search of them. He traveled all day and did not find them. He discovered a canyon that had a cave-like place where he could sleep. The snow fell in the night. When he awoke, the water had frozen. He built a fire in the cave and put a rock on the fire. The rock had a concave worn spot in it. He put the snow in this concave area of the rock and melted the snow. He drank this water, and it was good.

He heard a loud noise overhead. He went out of the cave and looked up in the sky. Above him were many crows flying back and forth over the canyon. This cave was the home of the crows. He called out to them, and other feathered people arrived. There was the chaparral cock as well.

He called out a blessing to them. Down in the canyon, he saw the many fires that had been made by the feathered people. He called out a song of respect to them. Two crows came up to him. They stood beside him, and he listened to hear what they were saying. The two crows cried out together, "There is one who speaks. There is one who speaks."

Two other crows landed and said, "What is your fear? What is your fear?"

The first two crows answered, "Two of us are no more. Two of us are no more. There were two men who appeared to be brothers, and they killed without blessings. Two of us are no more."

The last two crows shook their heads and asked, "What is to be done? What is to be done?"

The first two said, "These two travel around all the time, and they have killed twelve deer. A group of our people went to the deer after they were killed. Two of us who went after the blood of the deer were shot without a blessing."

The last two crows were very sad, and they asked, "Which men got killed? Which of the feathered people were killed?"

The first two said, "The chaparral cock who perched on the horn of the deer and the crow who pecked on the backbone of a deer."

The others cawed, "We are not safe when we go after the meat of a dead brother. It is a time when we can be killed as well. Death is near those who have been killed. It is to be expected."

The first two crows lifted their beaks. "We will not think of them any longer, for they have gone to the other world."

The crows flew off and disappeared into the thick, white clouds of the early morning. The gift-giver, storyteller brother sat and listened and thought on what had been said. After a time the feathered people on the other side of the canyon started to dance. They sang songs. The gift-giver, storyteller brother could not see clearly what they were doing, but he heard the song. After the dance, the feathered people made a great fire. He could see black objects moving through it, and he heard the voice of Hasjelti. He listened, and in his spirit he remembered every song, every movement, every meaning of this dance.

The feathered people danced back and forth until daylight. It was the ninth day when the gift-giving, storytelling brother decided to go back to the camp and tell his brothers what he had seen and learned. When he arrived at the camp, his brothers were there.

When they saw their brother, they shook their heads and said, "He will have lots of stories to tell. He will say he saw something that no one ever saw." The brothers clicked their tongues.

The oldest brother said, "Let him alone. I believe he really feels these things, for no one could make them up. I believe these stories to be true."

The brothers' camp was surrounded by piñon brush, and the fire burned in the center of the camp. Meat roasted over the fire. When the gift-giving, storytelling brother arrived, he raked over the coals and said, "I feel a great coldness here."

The older brother said, "It is cold tonight. It is good when people camp together, for then they can share stories and feel their spirits grow." They asked the gift-giving, storytelling brother to tell them of his story.

The brother said, "The feathered people told me of hunters who had killed twelve deer. The hunters then killed a chaparral jay and a crow that were on one of the dead deer. This was not good. The feathered people danced back and forth across the canyon out of sadness for what had happened. The hunters did not bless or pray before they killed the feathered people, and this was not good."

The brothers listened. They had killed twelve deer. They had killed two birds. The older brother said, "I will now be more thoughtful of you and will listen to your stories, for you have much to teach us."

They started back to their home. They started back to the place of the Navaho. As they walked down the canyon path, they saw many sheep winding their way down the canyon as well. The older brothers called to gift-giving, storytelling brother and told him to kill some sheep. The brothers who had hunted were tired. The gift-giving, storytelling brother took his bow and arrows and started after the sheep.

The sheep walked right to him as he hid behind the brush. The gift-giving, storytelling brother raised his bow, and with a prayer, he aimed at the sheep. But as he pulled the arrow back in the bow, his arm went limp and fell at his side. He could not shoot. He ran ahead and found another good hiding place. He lifted his bow, readied his aim, and pulled back on the bow. Again his arm went limp, and he could not shoot. This continued until the fourth time.

The fourth time that the brother raised his bow, his whole body went limp, and he fell into a deep sleep there behind a bush. The sheep approached the sleeping brother. As they came to him, they changed into the shape of great spirits. One became the spirit of Hasjelti; the second was Hostjoghon; the third was Naaskiddi; the fourth was Hadatchishi. Hasjelti stood to the east of the youth, Hostjoghon to the south, Naaskiddi to the west, and Hadatchishi to the north of him. Each of these great spirits had a rattle. They shook the rattle and sang to the brother. They traced in the sand with their rattles a symbol that meant man. When the symbol was drawn, the brother awoke and stood.

He looked around him. All he saw were sheep. The sheep asked him, "Why do you try to kill us?" The brother said nothing. The sheep then told him, "There is to be a dance far off to the north beyond Ute Mountain, and we want you to come with us to it. We will give you the dress that we wear and will teach you the dance that we dance. And then we will rise over the world."

The brothers waited for the gift-giving, storytelling brother. They could see him moving around way down below them, and they wondered what he was doing and why he was taking so long to shoot the sheep. They hurried down the mountain when they saw their brother fall. But when they arrived at that place, all they found was the figure drawn in the dirt. They found many sheep marks and started to cry, "He has gone off with the sheep. He tried to talk with us, tried to teach us, and we would not listen. Now he has gone off with the sheep!"

The gift-giving, storytelling brother learned songs, dances, prayers, and strength of spirit from the gathered sheep. The sheep people then decided to send the brother back to his people so that he could teach them the ways of the sheep. Hasjelti led the brother back to his people. He showed the people how to have the dances, how to sing the songs, and how to make masks to represent the sheep. This was done, and from it came the wisdom and the medicinal healing of the Sheep People. Animals and people, being as one, heal together with respect.

12. Healers on the Mountain

Wind That Grows stood beside the path. Her long brown hair was tangled from shoulder to waist. The forest was deeper in the dark. The animals were larger when their shapes were only shadows. The path from her home to her aunt's house had become longer with her fear.

The teeth in her pouch were held firmly in her hand. Teeth were all that she had left—four teeth and a spirit song. Her aunt would bring Raven Caller back to her. She knew of healings. She knew the ways of magic. These teeth were the only true proof she had of her man, her Raven Caller. His spirit was true, as true as her own. With this, magic could happen.

"Words of thought can stop the growth of life. Wonder with your heart or your eyes, but never with your mouth." Her mother's final words to her repeated in her head. Wind That Grows held firmly to the pouch. The teeth, the song, these would someday be her way out of her fateful path with an evil old woman and her evil ways. Wind That Grows pushed a hanging dead tree branch out of her way. She could see her aunt's home, there on the hill. She ran to it. Her aunt's home was deserted.

The long climb up the hill of sharp rock and through the old forest had caused her feet and hands to bleed, for she had fallen. But the joy and hope of seeing her aunt and having her help had moved her forward. Now she stood in front of the fallen mud walls and stared at the empty shell of a house. Her eyes teared only slightly as her heart filled with cold indifference. The wind blew, tossing her long brown hair around her face. Sun shone through the wandering black clouds.

Wind That Grows knelt down and picked up an old flint knife that lay in the debris. She hurt. The center of her being was on fire, and the pain was intense. She took the old flint knife and lifted it to her face. "AA-EEE-III-AAA!" She grabbed at her hair and cut it off, letting it be carried away on the wind. She cut her hair, chopping it shorter and shorter, letting her bloody fingers grab and drop her hair as she called out in her pain.

Wind That Grows searched the sky for a vision. No birds flew. No voice spoke to her. Wind That Grows moved in silence as she pushed forward across the plain. She knelt down on the sandy, moist earth and called out in her soft voice, "Where are you? Wise One, tell me what to do. Wise One, please be well, whole, and filled with life. Wise One, where are you?"

Silence echoed. Wind That Grows grasped the pouch in her hand, tugging at its leather thong around her neck. "Wise One, there is pain, such pain. Your healing is needed. Wise One, where are you?" Wind That Grows let her soft words be taken on the wind.

Sun shone, letting the black clouds of heavy rain cover his face. Sun could do nothing to help this one. The power of the healer who knows the way of the people was needed. Wind That Grows stood up, and her fine buckskin manta dress was now ripped, stained with blood, and ragged. Her eyes longed to see her Raven Caller. Her hand ached to touch his hand. She lifted up the leather pouch that held his four teeth and rubbed it against her cheek. "Oh, great spirits, ahhh. Great spirits, this pain burns deeply through my soul. Great spirits, give us strength. Give us hope. Help me find the healer."

Wind That Grows let the wind blow against her back. She studied the sky. No ravens, not a one—none to guide her, to show her where to go. There were only the dark, threatening clouds. The wind pushed against her back. "Wind, show me, show me where to go." The wind pushed her forward to the Mountain of Plumes. She did not know the path, for this was a sacred mountain, a mountain only for the wise men of the village. She let the wind push her to the path.

The high mesa that she walked across came to an end. In front of her was a cliff that led to a deep crevice, and on the other side was the Mountain of Plumes—the sacred mountain where the prayer feathers were placed and the plumes of fertility were left as blessings from the men so that they would have healthy families and fruitful women. Wind That Grows felt the wind pushing her forward. She studied the dropoff in front of her. It was ragged and steep. Her moccasins already were torn; her feet already were sore; and her hands were chapped from the hard, cold wind and blowing rain. She saw a way through the rocks where she could descend carefully.

She turned, facing the mountain, and carefully placed her foot down on a flat-headed boulder. Her hands grasped an indented lava rock that held her weight as she lowered herself down. The pouch with the teeth in it dangled from her neck on the leather thong. She worked her way down, slowly, foothold by foothold, hand by hand, level by level.

Suddenly, from a small niche in front of her, a mud swallow flew out and almost hit her. It struck her leather pouch and ripped it off her neck. Then the mud swallow was gone. Wind That Grows let fall the strength of her being. Her feet no longer reached for a flat rock, and her bloody fingers went limp. She wanted to call out to the sky, but her body fell, fell, rolling, banging, bouncing, until it hit the hard rock floor. She was broken, battered, bloody, and still. Silence was broken.

Ravens flew from all directions. Their screeching deafened the wind and terrified the dark clouds. Their wings beat at the air and churned the north wind, letting the clouds move with it. The ravens flew down, down, down, down, down to the battered body of Wind That Grows. They called out over her body, but there was no response. Magpie flew around, dropping spirit power over her. Wind That Grows did not move. There was only soft, labored breathing.

Mud Swallow flew over the mesa, over the path of deer, over the fast-flowing river, to the place of Smoking Cave. Mud Swallow flew into the thick-smoked cave, changing into Healing Woman. The strong, fast wings fell away to reveal old, brown, weathered arms. The talons became her wrinkled legs, and the tail fell away to reveal the hump on her back. Feathers became an old, worn, brown leather dress. This healer had bright, brown eyes of a bird and the magic of the spirits.

The leather pouch was carefully lifted to a bed of straw that had been prepared for it. Healing Woman opened the pouch. She let drop the four teeth, which were more than just teeth to her: they were the whole person. They were Raven Caller. She saw the strength of a hunter's arms, the power of a runner's legs, the smile of early dawn, the grey-green eyes that loved life, and the spirit that needed to be whole again.

Healing Woman pulled the eagle feather from its resting shelf. She laid it next to the teeth. Healing Woman pulled her weak legs under her; then she opened her mouth, and a song of life flowed from her lips. The song lifted the eagle feather, and it touched one tooth. The tooth moved; then the next tooth moved; and finally there was a circle of teeth gaining speed as they whirled into the shape of a young boy. The young boy floated to the highest level of the cave and hovered in the thick smoke. Song filled the cave. Song filled each membrane of the thick air. Song elevated the spirit of the boy into that of a man.

His voice joined hers. The two voices echoed in the small cave. The eagle feather danced in the thick air between them. Healing magic was strong here. Spirit strength grew. Spirit strength filled the cave, and when it stopped, there, standing in front of the healing woman, was Raven Caller. His strong hand touched Healing Woman's face.

"You are truly wise," he said. "You are the renewer of life. You are great in your ways, and this one thanks you."

Healing Woman bowed her head. She whispered to him, "Your woman brought you life. Your healing will save her."

Healing Woman fell back onto her bed of bird feathers. Raven Caller saw the tears of Healing Woman. Her fear touched his heart. He turned and left the cave. The cold snow melted upon his touch. Raven Caller searched the sky. He called out in a deep, rasping voice. The ravens came. They flew around his head. Magpie landed on his shoulder. They called to him, telling him of the way. He followed them. He followed them to the mesa, but he could not follow them down the steep cliff to the crevice where Wind That Grows lay barely breathing.

Raven Caller knelt upon the ground. He drew a circle starting in the north, then moving to the east, to the south, to the west. He backed up into the center of the circle. He started another circle, drawing from the south, to the west, to the north, to the east. He lifted dirt from the earth toward the sky.

"Wind that blows, find Wind That Grows and tell her that we are coming to help her. We are on our way to her." He let the dirt fall, and the wind blew it down the cliff to the place where Wind That Grows lay.

Raven Caller studied the sky. He had plenty of time to run back to the village where Wind That Grows' family lived. Raven Caller told the ravens to watch his woman and keep her safe from harm. He loped along the mesa to the south. The village loomed up at the base of another mesa. The night fires were being started as he ran to Wind That Grows' home.

Wind That Grows' father sat in front of his medicine pouch. He was picking out items that he would need for healing. He did not look up when Raven Caller entered the room.

"You have brought this to my daughter," he said. "Raven Caller, your evil past has brought this to my daughter. You are the one who has hurt her."

Raven Caller sat to the left of the father. "It is my doing," he said. "My wish was not to hurt your daughter; my wish was to be with her forever."

The father turned his head but remained looking down. "You have come for help. You wish me to help you get to my daughter. You cannot be with my daughter until you deal with the evil that still exists in your life. You are still threatened by the evil one. Your testing is to have her removed from your life."

Raven Caller stood up. He felt the anger rise in his heart. "The evil one is not here. She cannot hurt us now. She is gone."

The father stood, and turning his back on Raven Caller, he said again, "You are still threatened by the evil one. Your testing is to have her removed from your life."

Raven Caller walked out of the house. He walked away from the village. His being felt the hurt of Wind That Grows. His mind knew that the evil one was responsible for this, not he.

Raven Caller called out to his ravens. They flew down to him. "Find me the evil one," he said. "Find her, and then guide me to her place of dwelling."

The ravens flew away. Raven Caller walked to a small cave in the side of a hill near the village. He found his medicine pouch there, his sacred corn meal, and his feathers. He put the feathers in his hair, the pouch around his neck, and the corn meal he rubbed on his face and hands and feet. The ravens returned.

Raven Caller found the evil one. She was fattened with her wealth. She had taken all that he once had. He had believed once that she was his caretaker. She had found him when he was young, battered, and just learning of life. She had raised him to do exactly as she ordered. If he wavered from her demands, she punished him severely. She once had held all that he was in her power, but he had run away. He found that he could not breathe near her, that he could not think near her, and that he could not live with her anymore. He had taken what was most precious to him and had run to the cave in the hill. His strength had been his survival, and the village people had accepted him.

His life had been fairly well established, and the evil one had left him alone—except that every now and then she would call him names in the village or would break his spirit if he felt too good. Otherwise, she left him alone.

Then he met Wind That Grows and fell in love with her. The evil one grew angry, angry enough to destroy him. The evil one set about making Raven Caller sick. Then she called him to her, saying that she was dying and needed him. Raven Caller had gone to her, believing that she was truly ill. The evil one had trapped Raven Caller and, in one moment of her wicked magic, believed that she had killed him.

Raven Caller had felt his spirit grow weak. He felt the power of life leaving him. With strong fingers he ripped out his front four teeth and threw them out of the evil one's home to be carried by the raven to Wind That Grows. He fell into an unseen cloud. The evil one was proud and let the unseen cloud float out of the window. Raven Caller was taken by the wind to the Healing Woman, and there he had waited for her magic to begin.

Now, the evil one stood outside her doorway. She understood the birds, and she knew of his coming. Raven Caller walked up to this evil one who held power. In one hand she had corn meal of the ancient ones, and in the other hand she held a lock of his hair. Raven Caller did not stop but walked straight up to her and touched her face.

"You thought you had power to kill," he said. "You thought you had the power to make me into whatever you wanted me to be, but you have done better than that. You have allowed me to be my own person, to believe what I choose, and to find freedom and strength by trying to defeat me. You have given me the greatest gift of all, knowledge of myself."

Raven Caller looked into her angry eyes, and then he turned and walked away. He walked down the hill, through the village, and out across the mesa.

Raven Caller caught up with Father. The two men walked side by side to the edge of the cliff. Birds hovered all around them as they slowly and carefully descended the cliff face. Father moved with great ease, for he was one of the elders who went to Mountain of Plumes every year. Raven Caller followed Father's path. They found Wind That Grows at the bottom of the crevice. She was covered with magpies and ravens who were sheltering her body from the ice-cold wind.

Father took his medicine pouch off his neck and opened it wide. He carefully took out each item. He chanted as he placed each thing in its power place. Raven Caller stood and watched as the ravens sat on his shoulders. Wind That Grows slowly opened her eyes. She looked up into the sky and saw Raven Caller.

Father took corn meal and rubbed it over her eyes, across her nose, over her lips. Father lifted her hands and rubbed her body.

"She is broken," he said. "Her back and her legs are broken. We need to get her home and cared for. Come, Raven Caller, we need to make a carry for her."

Raven Caller lifted his pouch from his neck. He stood over her, and with his hands raised high in the sky, he called all the birds. There was a blast of noise as birds filled all the air around them. Father huddled down next to his daughter.

"Ravens, crows, magpie, blue-jays, piñon jays, sparrows, mud-swallows, robins, hummingbirds, eagles, hawks, red-wings, all come, all come and help me in my song." Raven Caller took the sacred powder from his pouch and threw it high into the air. The birds sang as they hovered over Wind That Grows. Her fingers stretched, her arms moved, her legs stretched, her feet moved, and she sat upright. Father knelt back on his feet.

Wind That Grows stood up and reached for Raven Caller. "Are you real? Are you really here?"

Raven Caller took her hand, saying, "It is time to go home."

Father collected his sacred items. He took the two feathers that were tucked into his belt and said, "These belong on the mountain. These need to be placed there by you." He handed a feather to each one of them.

Father worked his way back up the cliff face to the village. Behind him, he could hear Wind That Grows and Raven Caller climb up the mountain. They never came down. They are still there, healing those in need. This place is called Healers on the Mountain.

13. Guiana Medicine and the Crows

Makanauro was a very clever man. He was known as a *semi-chichi*, or a medicine man. He would go out and set his traps in the bush. He was always catching something, whether bird or animal. Then a time came when he would go out to find that someone had broken his trap and taken the catch. This annoyed him. He studied the trap area. There were no marks around it. There were no footprints around it. There were no broken branches. There was no sign of who this thief could be. He stood puzzled by this.

Makanauro climbed a tree. He watched his traps. A black carrion crow came swooping down and tried to cut up the net with a knife and remove the animal. The crow's knife was too dull, so he flew away. Makanauro stayed in the tree and waited. The crow returned with Vulture, who had a sharper knife and cut up the animal nicely. More crows came down and cleared away every particle of the meat, leaving the net empty. Makanauro watched from his hiding place. He saw them go to his next net and watched Vulture cut up the meat, as before, while the carrion crows took it away.

Makanauro made up his mind to catch Vulture. Makanauro disguised himself with cotton binding and lay down next to one of the net traps. He remained perfectly still. The crow came down first, but his knife was still too blunt to do any damage to Makanauro. So the crow went to find Vulture, but when that bird came quite close to Makanauro, he seized it. This scared away all the other crows.

Vulture was a hen bird. Makanauro held her in his hands and found her to be very enticing. He married her there at that place. They lived well together for many years. The carrion crows returned to live nearby and visited them.

One day, Vulture Wife sent Makanauro to fetch some water, which he had to find at the river. He tried to catch the water in the "quake" that Vulture Wife had given him, but the water would not stay in it, flowing out instead through the mesh work. Makanauro tried several times, but it would not work. He was becoming very frustrated.

Some Muneri ants noticed the dance Makanauro did trying to keep the water in the quake. The Muneri ants asked him to teach them the dance, and in exchange they would patch the quake with an ant bed. Makanauro showed them how he dipped the quake in the water, how he dipped it down to catch the water, how he lifted it fast, and how the water dripped all down him. The Muneri ants learned these movements quickly and proceeded to patch the quake.

Makanauro returned home with the quake filled with water. Vulture Wife was very impressed. She now believed that her man was a medicine man and magic in his ways. As time passed, however, she began to wonder about him. She decided to test him a second way. She sent him out to cut a field for her. He was not to return until all the bushes, trees, vines, and grasses had been cut down.

Makanauro worked all day in the field. He worked hard until the sweat fell from his body, like water from the falls. Yet in the morning, when he went back out to the field, all the bushes, trees, vines, and grasses were standing again. Vulture Wife had called to the carrion crows, and they were going out to the field at night and lifting the cut bush, trees, vines, and grasses back up to grow again. Poor Makanauro did not know what to do.

Makanauro talked to the Kushi ants and asked them to eat up all the wood, branches, and leaves as fast as he could cut them down. They saw the sadness in his face, and they agreed to help him. The carrion crows could not fight against the Kushi ants. Makanauro completed the clearing of the field. Vulture Wife was again filled with pride that her man was a medicine man—perhaps.

Vulture Wife decided that she would test Makanauro a third time. She sent him out to make a chair bench for Mother-in-Law. He was told to carve the head of the chair bench in an exact likeness of Mother-in-Law herself. This task Vulture Wife thought impossible. Makanauro thought so, too, for he had never seen Mother-in-Law. He tried to find out what she looked like, but when he looked in the direction of the old woman, she covered her face with her shawl or turned aside so he could not see her face. He became frustrated.

Makanauro thought awhile and had an idea. He climbed on the top of her roof and hung down over the place where she sat by the fire. He gathered up some centipedes and let them fall into her lap. This made her lift her arms and look up to see from where the centipedes fell, and she showed him her face.

Makanauro cut the wood for the chair bench. He trimmed it into the right shape and then carved two excellent likenesses of her as two heads—one on each side of the chair bench. Vulture Wife then took the chair bench to Mother-in-Law. Vulture Wife was impressed with the work her husband had done, and now she believed him to be a medicine man.

Vulture Wife could not be pleased for long. She sent out Makanauro to gather some fish for her. He brought her a package he said was filled with fish. She studied the small package and said that there were not enough fish in the package for her and that he should go out and bring more.

He sat back and smiled. "Open the package," he said, "and then tell me that you need more fish."

Vulture Wife opened the package, and the fish fell from it and multiplied and multiplied until the room was filled with fish. Makanauro laughed and laughed, for this was good.

Vulture Wife gave birth to a son. She was proud of this boy. She wanted to show off her medicine-man husband and her fine boy to her people. She told Makanauro that they had to leave, for she must go to her father's above the clouds. They went there and remained with her family and the carrion crows. Vulture Wife bragged about Makanauro, and perhaps she said things that were not altogether true.

The crows asked Makanauro to perform some impossible tasks. He did these. This made the crows angry at his power, and they became jealous. The crows decided that they would kill Makanauro, for he was too wise and too clever. Makanauro knew of their plans. He told the crows that he wanted to go back down to his people, who would fight the crows. He returned to his old home, and he collected all the birds that he knew. He told them to prepare for a battle with the carrion crows.

When they arrived and the crows saw all the other birds, they became frightened and decided to plan a technique that would bring them victory. Their idea was to burn up the whole world. Makanauro and his friends would all burn in the fire. The carrion crows thought this idea very clever.

The black Kurri-kurri birds were flying high and heard these plans. They told Makanauro. Makanauro called the birds to him as the fires started to burn all around them. Makanauro and the birds began to dance and sing, and the rains came and put out the fires. Vulture Wife was angered by her husband's cleverness in defeating her people and friends. She called the other vultures to her and told them to fall down to the earth and destroy Makanauro and his friends. Whether they did this, I do not know.

Healing Myths

Life song, life strong, life flowing from within is all growing. Growing sound, good, pure, and in good health is the goal of the birthing mother to her infant. Whole, sound, safe, and fed in good health—father to wife to child. Harmony of love, life, health, goodness, and deep peace, the balance strong. Harmony comes from the depth of feeling. Feel your harmony strong and deep within you. Feel the disharmony when life is not right—feel it.

Native American tradition has it that you are born good, whole, pure, and as you should be—good to be good all your days, whole in ceremony and truth, pure in all that you do, and as you should be without question. Yet there is imbalance. Outside forces pull, jerk, tear, rip, sear, or lean on you. When the time is right, you will hear, feel, and know that you need healing to find harmony.

Harmony and healing are one to the other the same. Healing comes in different forms and can be reached through anger, terror, fear, love, hand holding, or whatever a culture believes is a cure. To heal is the goal; to maintain the harmony is next; and to sustain the healed state is the way of life. Many cultures have concepts that come with their own story. Here are their stories.

1. Guiana Healers

Some people were helped by the healing pattern of the fire. When a person was very sick and the cause was unknown, he or she was placed in the middle of a fire-lit area. A great fear would enter the person who was ill. A Makusi medicine man would come out of his hut with two large, round bundles of leaves and would yell at the people outside the fires.

He would whip out the fires, howling as he extinguished them. After a time someone would answer his howl from the other side of the hammocks that were strung on the trees outside the fire area. He would then light up a cigar and blow the foul smoke into the face of the person who was ill, making the patient cough and sputter. He would take the bundle of smoldering leaves and press them against the forehead of the sick person, who would yell and call out. He would do this for quite a long period, and when it was time for him to leave, the sick person would be well.

Magic has many different forms and is used in healing throughout the Americas. Here is a story of Guiana magic people:

It is believed that there were once two nations—one of them keeping the Dwarfs, who were small as little children. They were called the Guayazis, and they had come into the world with their feet turned behind them so that those who did not know them would follow their tracks and go away rather than toward them.

The other nation was called Matayus, and they came from the tributary of Toupinambous and used stone hatchets to fell great trees. When they had made up their minds to clear the land, they did it quickly.

Up the Cunuris River, on the north side of the great Amazon and to the east of the Toupinambou Island, lived the Apotos, the

Taguaus, and the Guacaras. They had the privilege to talk with the valiant women and enjoy their favors. They lived on the huge mountains. There was one peak that lifted its head high above the village of Yacamiaba, where the valiant women lived alone without the help of men. The valiant women confronted their neighbors with bows and arrows of war. But once the valiant women saw that they were peaceful people, they put down their weapons.

The valiant women would reach into their canoes and take out their hammocks. Once their hammocks were hung from the tall trees, they would beckon to their visitors. Valiant women pampered their guests and knew of healing techniques. Male guests were given special attention. If female children were born, they were raised by the valiant women. If male children were born, no one ever saw them.

The Orinoco had a hairy man of the woods. He was called the Salvaje. He carried off women, built huts, and ate humans. The Tamanacs called him *achi,* and the Maypures called him *vasitri,* or devil man. He was believed to be shaped like a monkey man. This hairy man finally found a woman who had as much hair as he did, and he settled down and left the people alone. This woman used unusual healing techniques, and people came to her for her cures. The missionaries tried to get her to come to church with her children, but she felt uncomfortable and returned to her man, never to be seen again.

The Guiana had a medicine man who was short and hairy, jumping wherever he went. His name was Koneso. Koneso was a rabbit, or so some thought. It could be he was short, hairy, and jumped but was really a man. He traveled all over the country and had children everywhere he went. He gave trouble to the single women and upset the harmony of many a married man's home. The other men would try to club him or shoot him with an arrow, but it would glide off him or break, and Koneso would laugh and laugh. But Koneso soon got tired.

The country to which he traveled was ruled by a proud *nafudi,* boss man or chieftain. This nafudi had a very beautiful daughter known for her purity. Koneso happened to see this lovely woman one day and asked if he could marry her. The nafudi told Koneso that he must first bring him two quakes full of alligator and *camudi* eyes.

Koneso tried to make the quakes, and he spent many days arranging for the bait to catch the alligators. He took the meat down to the river bank. He took his bone flute and played pretty music. The alligators and the camudis came out of the water to listen. He then handed them the meat and with it some drinks that he had put in a calabash. This made them all drunk, and while they were lying around, he gouged out their eyes with his sharp finger.

He filled his homemade quakes with their eyes and hurried back to the nafudi.

But the nafudi said, "I cannot let anyone like you have my daughter. You are unclean." Then the nafudi bent over and pulled on Koneso's ear. Then he pulled on the other ear. He pulled so hard that Koneso's ears got stretched, and now he has long ears. Koneso became very angry, and he told the nafudi that he would get his daughter and would show him a trick or two.

Koneso waited for the pretty daughter to go out and relieve herself. When she did this, he would jump on top of her and try to take liberties with her. The nafudi found him and beat him, but the stick he used broke into many pieces when it touched Koneso.

When the nafudi saw that he could not hurt Koneso this way, he ordered his round men to seize Koneso. They did so and tied him to a tree, then shot at him with bows and arrows at close range. But every arrow they shot broke or glanced off him.

Next, the men put Koneso in a corral and tied him to the benches there. They put up a sail and let the vessel drift out to sea. Koneso soon released himself and sailed back again. He went to the nafudi and told him that he had brought the boat back safely into port.

The men seized Koneso a third time. They bound him hand and foot, fixed a long vine rope around his neck, tied the rope to a stone, and threw him in the sea. But as soon as Koneso touched the bottom, he freed himself and walked up the sea floor to the open beach. He went to the nafudi and told him that he had brought the stone back and it was safe. The nafudi let Koneso have his daughter.

Koneso became homesick. He left his nafudi family and returned to the deep forest. One day, deep in the forest, Koneso pulled up a big vine rope. Tiger heard the vine rope move. Tiger followed the sound and came to Koneso. Tiger asked Koneso what he was doing.

"Nothing," said Koneso, "except that there will be a big wind blowing the day after tomorrow, and I don't want to be blown away. I will use this vine to tie myself up, and I will be safe."

Tiger worried about this and asked Koneso to tie him up first. Koneso tied up the tiger and walked home again. Tiger waited patiently for the blowing wind. Tiger waited for many days. Tiger then waited for Koneso to come and untie him. Tiger began to feel hungry. Tiger tried to pull himself loose, but he could not. Many animals passed by, and Tiger begged each and every one of them to undo the ropes. But they were afraid, for if free, Tiger might eat them. At last, on the fourth day, a carrion crow came hopping along, and Tiger promised that if the bird let him go, he never would eat a carrion crow again. The crow released him, and to this day the tiger will not eat a carrion crow.

The tiger and the carrion crow hold many healing powers of the people.

2. Wolverine's Sister

A young wolverine wandered away from home. He could not find any food, and he became very hungry and desperate. As he walked along, he called out to the animals in the forest. He called for a brother or a friend to help him find food. A tall bear ambled up to him and asked, "What is it? Why are you calling out?"

The wolverine cautiously approached the bear. "Are you my sister?" he asked. The bear sat back. "I did not know that I had a brother. Are you my brother?"

The bear turned and ran away, and the wolverine ran after, calling, "Do not run away. Our father has sent me to find you. You were lost when you were little while out picking berries. I have come to find you and to take you home."

The bear slowed down and eventually stopped. The wolverine ran up to the bear. "I have come to find you." The bear turned and studied the wolverine. "Don't you know of the place on the hill that has all the nice, round, sweet, tender berries?" The bear studied the wolverine, then nodded her head. "Yes."

The wolverine continued, "Do you see the berries on the hill?"

The bear answered, "It is a great distance from here."

The wolverine smiled. "Come, I will show you close up. If you have been there, then you know of the berries that I speak of. Come."

The bear followed the wolverine and asked, "How is it that you can see the berries if they are so far away?"

The wolverine quietly answered, "It was the berries. When I was very young, Father crushed the berries into my eyes."

The bear was curious. "Father crushed berries into your eyes?"

"Yes. Come, I will crush berry juice into *your* eyes, and you can see far, far, far, far."

The bear followed the wolverine. They came to the berries on the hill. It was dark, and the moon only allowed some light to show their position.

The wolverine asked the bear, "Would you look around for a good sharp stone? It needs to be very sharp so that we can crush berries and put them in your eyes." The bear stumbled around and was more interested in the berries.

The wolverine patted the bear. "You pick the berries, and I will get the stone."

Bear did not answer, for she was busy eating the berries. Wolverine prepared a sweat house, and in the center was a very sharp rock concealed under some moss and twigs.

Bear followed the wolverine into the sweat house. They did their sweat. Wolverine took the bear outside.

"Bear, it is now time for the berry juice. I could not find a very sharp rock, but this flat one will do." Wolverine crushed the berries and poured juice in the bear's eyes.

The bear cried out, "This hurts! This hurts! I cannot do this! It hurts!"

Wolverine patted the bear. "You are too good a sister," he said. "Wait, and I will help you."

Wolverine went into the sweat house and picked up the sharp, hot rock with the soft, cool moss. Wolverine stood over the bear, who was crying out in pain. Wolverine smashed in the bear's skull and killed her.

The bear might not have come to this end had she worn *sutsig'in,* also known as horsemint. The sutsig'in is used as a treatment for protection and clarity. The dried leaves are taken internally, and, at the same time, a few also are enclosed in a narrow strip of deerskin worn around one's neck for protection and clear thinking.

3. Thunder Being

The Omaha and the Ponka tell of their battles, which could only be fought when the Thunder Being was present. The Omaha People called the Black Bear People, and they went to the Elk People. The Elk People called upon Thunder Being.

The Ponka People called the Black Bear People. The Black Bear People called, *"Han,i'c'age, eitucapa an gat'a!"* ["Loud One, bring your club and beat it against the sky!"]

Thunder Being still is called. Thunder Being brings magic to ceremony, as he did to the people when they were on a warpath. Thunder Being was known as Nuda-hanga, or war captain. His spiritual magic combined the reality of materialism and spirituality, which brought about a special state of energy. The circle of life is not just physical, but empowered and alive. From this unity, a person can remain whole and healed in ceremony or battle.

4. Arapaho Woman and the Butterflies

*Butterflies hold the ability to go from person to person, listening,
understanding, and moving on. The butterfly is like a healer
through stories, both listening and telling. Here, then, is a story
of a butterfly that brought a curious person to an undetermined
fate:*

There was a young woman, a beautiful and discontented
woman, who lived in a village. She asked questions and rarely
heard an answer that appeased her. People were irritated with
her frustration at their responses and had a tendency to avoid
her. This caused her to become more agitated and disagreeable.

Her man, who found her beautiful but difficult, would go
to his hunting and enjoy the silence away from home. Her young
baby would cry incessantly and was never quiet, even with her
mother's rocking, nursing, and walking. Life in the home was
difficult at best.

One day, this young woman became tired of waiting for her
man to come home. She would sit and rock the crying baby and
wait and wait. Her man was gone for days, and she never knew
when he would return, or if he would return, or if he would be
pleasant to her, and she decided to let him return to an empty
home rather than wait.

She wrapped the baby in the cradle board. She put some
dried jerky in her belt and a small sap-coated basket filled with
water in her pouch. She took a sharp knife, one of her man's
hunting knives, to use for cutting willow or other wood. She set
out on her trek.

She found a large amount of wood right away on this cool
fall day. She stacked it under a tall cottonwood tree that she could

easily find on her way home. She continued to search for more wood, stacking it at easy landmarks to recover later. The fall sun grew warm, and by mid-day it was comfortable. The woman put her heavy cradle board with her sleeping child down under a pine tree. The baby slept, quiet and peaceful at last. She walked away and stretched her back, relieved to have the heavy bundle off her body.

A large black butterfly flitted around her head. It flew to her face and almost landed on her full lips. She thought of swatting it, but she tasted the sweet flavor of its presence. Her face smiled with ecstacy. She reached out to catch the black, buoyant butterfly, but it flew out of her reach. She raced after it, but it continued to outdistance her. She ran for quite a distance, eager for its taste. She ran until her legs tired. She threw herself down under a tall aspen tree high up in the mountains. She looked down. She had run quite a distance. She squinted to find the tree under which she had placed her baby but could not make out which one it was.

She thought of standing up and going back, but her legs were tired and her feet sore from running. She let her head fall back on the aspen trunk. The sun felt good against her cheeks and forehead. She soon fell sound asleep.

The black butterfly flew around her face. The black butterfly landed on her mouth, letting fresh pollen from his body fall onto her open, well-rounded red lips. The woman licked her lips in her sleep. Her body felt warm. She slipped down to a horizontal position, and the butterfly flitted over her. The black butterfly dropped his pollen on her neck, on her arms, on her legs. The butterfly flitted his wings against her shoulder.

The maiden, in her sleep, lifted her right hand and untied her manta. She pulled it down and off of her body, never opening her eyes, never ceasing to lick her lips and to taste the delicious flavor of the pollen. The black butterfly touched her breasts, touched her belly, flitted down her thighs, and placed his pollen into her being. The maiden smiled in her sleep and continued to lick her lips. The black butterfly finished with his magic and flew away.

The maiden awoke. She jerked to a sitting position. Her eyes were serious as she found her manta lying beside her. She became alarmed and quickly drew it on, tying it over her shoulder. She stood up and looked about her. There was no one, only the sweet aroma that she longed for. She stared out across the land. There was the black butterfly flitting from bush to bush. She ran after that black butterfly. She ran after that black butterfly, intent on catching it and keeping it for her pleasure alone.

She ran and ran and ran and ran. She ran down into a meadow, and there, all around her, were thousands of black butterflies. They flitted around her head, around her hands, around her body. They were there but out of reach. She raced after them, frantically searching for the one that had brought her so much pleasure. They all looked alike. They all appeared to be the same. She turned around and around and around and around, desperate for the one black butterfly that she desired.

The baby cried. The baby cried and cried and cried. Its lips were chapped from the hot sun beating down. The child tried to move, but it was tied tightly in the cradle board. The cradle board would not fall over, nor lie flat. The baby was hungry and wanted to nurse, and it was thirsty.

The people heard the child's tired cries as they searched over the mountain. Four days had passed, and the baby still persistently called out for food. The people gave it fresh goat's milk. They untied it and cared for it. The high winds at night had chafed the baby's face and arms. But the child had been wrapped warmly and was otherwise fine. The people searched for the mother's footprints. They could find none. They continued their search for four more days.

The woman was never found. A new mother cared for the baby. The father became a quiet, peaceful man.

The black butterflies have never been seen since that time, though the people do say that the butterflies are waiting to come again.

5. Kotcininako

The people continued to increase on Old Earth Woman. The Tewa Pueblo people were slowly moving around, learning more and more of this place. There was not enough food because the fields were being used too much and too often. The rain was coming every day, and the people danced every day.

The Sacred Sisters realized that the crops were not enough to feed the people. Uretsiti decided that she would create all kinds of game animals. Uretsiti called for the sacred manta of life. Uretsiti laid the manta out on the ground and brought forth animals to be hunted by the people. She gave to each animal a life, habits, and a place to live.

The men of the White-House Place were called to see the animals and to recognize them as beings to be hunted for food. Tools for the hunt were developed. Some of these tools were developed to kill people. There was trouble. Trouble continued, and there was no one to help deal with this much trouble.

Tsityostinako and Uretsiti had a meeting. Tsityostinako decided that a woman of humility, kindness, and honor was needed to bear leaders who could stop the trouble. Uretsiti agreed, and a baby girl was born. A daughter was born to an officer of the pueblo and his woman.

This daughter was hard-working, beautiful, and very humble. She learned the skills of womanhood from her wise mother. This daughter would indeed be a good woman for a good man. This proud woman, however, would not have anything to do with men. They offered her gifts and promises, but she turned away. She refused all of them. Her father argued with the men that his daughter was not yet ripe for life. Her mother worked very hard teaching her daughter to be humble, to work with pride, and to be loyal to the family traditions.

Each spring the young men came. Many young men held great prestige and honor in the village. Some held fruitful fields, while others held the richness of spirit knowledge. The young woman turned them all away.

Sadness entered the mother's spirit—a sadness that her daughter would not be content with life, that her daughter was chosen for a painful testing. The mother aged in her grief; and as she aged, her daughter ground cornmeal more often. The daughter proudly carried the bowls of cornmeal to her parents. They no longer praised her hard work, however. Her mother scorned her daughter's labor, and the father soon lost interest in her existence.

One particular spring morning, very early, the daughter started to grind cornmeal. By mid-day, she had grown very tired. Her arms were heavy and her soul felt empty. She leaned against the door opening. The loneliness swelled up inside her. The daughter went outside and lay down on the sun-warmed soil. Sun climbed higher in the sky. His rays fell upon her body. The rays filled her with warmth. Sun filled her saddened spirit with strength.

Soon she awoke. The daughter felt renewed and went back to her grinding. She no longer tried to please her parents. She talked to the turkeys as she walked them across the plains for food. She carefully watched over them as she put them in the pen at evening light. Somehow, the daughter no longer felt connected to these people or this place. The tall, dark mesas with their long shadows filled her with curiosity. The colors of the dawn called to her.

With each dawn the daughter grew very plump. Everyone wondered at this. Soon there was no doubt that she was with child. The people knew children were born to those who had been blessed. They knew the blessings came from having humility, a pure heart, and a good man to provide for the woman and the child. This daughter, they felt, had few of these qualities.

The mother's illness began to subside. The father began to bring his daughter special items. The daughter watched them with care. The presents and the thoughtfulness increased. Talk

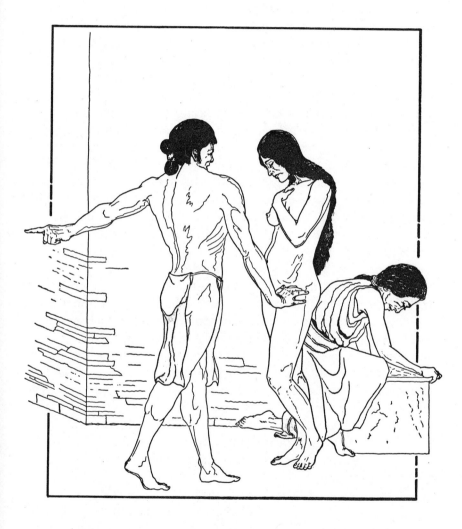

KOTGININAKO

always led to questions about who the daughter was seeing, who the provider man could be.

The daughter was angered at this. Not all women could be blessed with new life, even if they did see the fertility stars on the horizon. Her new life was a true blessing from the spirits, for she did not believe that she needed a man to provide for her. The mother begged her to tell them who the father of the child was. She shook her head and told them nothing, for she did not know. The men, who before had helped her carry water or corn, now clucked their tongues at her. Her father and mother were not asked to go on village hunting or gathering trips anymore.

Her father was an officer, and his daughter was taking away his respect. Early one morning, the father ordered his daughter to the front room of their home. The daughter came to the front room as requested. Her eyes stared at her father with coldness. He demanded that she tell him who had sired the child she carried. She looked at the floor, as was the sign of respect and humility. Her mother sat quietly in the corner of the room.

The father then pulled back the door blanket and told her to stand outside. She did as she was told. The mother reached up to her daughter's manta dress and pulled it loose. The mother said, "You shall feel the disgrace that you have placed upon us."

The daughter's manta dress fell to her feet. Her nakedness was bared to all the village people. The mother told her to turn and bend over. Her mother said this loudly for everyone to hear: "Bend over and show the people that you are filled with life! Show them how you are!"

The father raised his voice and spoke, more to the people than to his daughter. "Go, my daughter, go and leave us. Go naked, and may the provider who brought you the gift of life come forward and show his honor and pride by protecting you and caring for you."

The daughter walked through the people. She held her head straight and her shoulders high. She moved through the people as they parted for her. She moved forward, for she was the carrier of life. She walked to the west by the turkey pens. She wanted to turn and pet the turkeys, but the people watched her, and she knew she must keep walking. She loved these turkeys as her own heart, for she had always been able to speak with them. They appeared to understand her feelings.

The young woman went up to the ash pile on the west side of the village. The sound of the people's voices now was a whisper. The young woman heard a clucking sound behind her, but she did not turn around. The turkeys were following her. When they reached her, one of the turkeys said, "Mother, hit me on the neck, hard."

The young woman was startled. She turned away, trying to hide her nakedness. Her large belly, rich with life, bulged beneath her. She spoke to the turkey. "You are my friend. Why do you follow me? Why do you want me to hit you?"

The turkey clucked sternly at her. "We are not here to judge what has happened. Do as I ask."

The young woman hit the turkey on the neck with the stick. The turkey clucked louder. "Hit me harder!"

The young woman held her large belly with one hand and with the other lifted the stick high into the air. She hit the turkey's neck very hard. The turkey stumbled and coughed up a manta.

The young woman backed away from the manta. "What is this?" she asked. "What have you done?"

The turkey clucked at her, "There is nothing we can do about your man, but we can help to clothe you. This is a manta dress for you to wear."

The young woman tried to bend over, but her body was too full. The turkey picked up the manta in its beak and gave it to the young woman. The young woman stroked the turkey's head. "Thank you," she said. "The manta dress is beautiful."

The young woman knew that this was great magic. She was pleased with the manta and put it on her body. A second turkey came and asked her to hit *it* on the neck. The young woman was hesitant, but the turkey insisted. She hit the turkey hard on the neck, and it began to sputter, coughing up a woven belt.

The young woman went through the same procedure with a third turkey, who coughed up moccasins and leggings, and a fourth turkey, who coughed up strings of beads. The turkeys then left her to her journey and returned to the village. Sun shone high in the sky.

The young woman continued walking toward the west. Her traveling was difficult. The life within her was moving lower down between her hips. The passage between her legs was being pushed open. Her breasts hurt and were ripe with milk. She moved with the sun guiding her. She was not sure where she was or where she would be going. Tears fell from her eyes.

Sun moved across the sky, being pulled to the house of night. Sun watched as the woman carrying his life sadly walked on into the night. The young woman stumbled in the darkness. She was hungry and tired, but she felt that she was needed somewhere else and that her journey was not yet over. Soon she came upon an older woman sitting by a small fire, waiting for someone.

The old woman called out, "Kotcininako, where are you going? I have been waiting for you. Where are you going now?"

The young woman turned and looked for the person to whom the old woman spoke. The old woman pointed her finger. She said, "You, you are known as Kotcininako. I have named you that. Where are you going? You should not be out wandering around, for you are with life and are soon to let it go free!"

Kotcininako lowered her head in respect. "Yes, my parents sent me from my home because I could not tell them how I became filled with this life."

The old woman got up and walked to Kotcininako. "Yes, I know. I know all that. But now, you need a place to stay. Come and stay with me in my home. I will care for you."

They walked to a hole in the flat ground. The hole was as large as a fist. Kotcininako studied this hole. The old woman comforted her. "Do not fear what you do not understand. Walk into the hole. Put your foot here and walk into the hole."

Kotcininako stepped forward, almost falling. She leaned back to balance, and the old woman caught her. Kotcininako cried out, "The life within me is falling. Soon it will come!"

The older woman clicked her tongue against her teeth. "You are filled with the richness of life. I am only an old woman, but I am wise. Trust me, for we will bring the life from within you here to this place. It will be good, for you are strong. I am strong. We will be strong together."

The hole in the ground became larger, larger, and larger until it was the size of a door. They went inside. The old woman put Kotcininako in her own room with a bedroll, fresh bread, and some water. Kotcininako stayed in the room for three days.

The third night, the old woman brought in baskets coated with hard tree pitch. The baskets were filled with water. One of the baskets had yucca water in it. The old woman washed Kotcininako's hair, arms, belly, legs, fingers, and feet with the yucca water. The old woman then took the clear water and washed Kotcininako's breasts and passage.

On the fourth morning, Kotcininako's passage began to open fully. Kotcininako cried out, "There should be a *tsaiyawaiya yayatitcra* here with the prayer meal. The baby needs the fetish and the tea ... three women to push down....",

The old woman laughed softly. "I am here. I am as strong as three. I have the knowledge of the *tsaiyawaiya yayatitcra*, and the prayer meal is here by your leg. The Kotcininako fetish is the manta dress that you wear; the belt that binds it; and the leggings, moccasins, and beads given to you by the turkeys. The spirit strength in this room is very strong, strong as the life spirits that light the sky."

Kotcininako turned her head aside. "Where is the father who brought about the germination inside me? His strength needs to nourish the spirit of this new one. He is needed to keep life growing in spirit. My milk is rich, but my spirit is not...."

The old woman brushed Kotcininako's hair back from her face. "We are the women who are here. We are here now. We must do with what we have. Now push, and let this spirit be free to its own choosing."

Kotcininako drank the tea. She squatted, letting the old woman push down on her large belly. The water of life washed out of the passage, clearing the path for the new life. Her legs were stretched and burning. The new life within her was strong and forceful as it pushed out into this place. The old woman reached down and caught the new one.

The son born was strong, kicking, and hungry. Kotcininako picked up the wet baby. She held it to her breast as the old woman continued to push on her belly. The squatting position was

difficult. Her legs were burning and tired. They waited for the life that followed. The newborn boy suckled slowly on her sore, plump breasts.

Then again the burning started. The old woman gave Kotcininako more tea. Kotcininako felt the spirit strength fill her, and she pushed hard. Harder. She pushed as hard as she could, holding the new one to her breast. She bore another son.

This one was quiet. His eyes were large and round. He was not as red as the first one. Kotcininako lifted this one to her other breast. This second one sucked forcefully on her breast, coughing and sputtering as he struggled for more. The milk flowed from her freely, relieving the pressure. The old woman continued to rub down on Kotcininako's belly. The belly flattened, and the life that followed poured out onto the ground.

Kotcininako then lay back and let the old woman perform the ceremony. The old woman placed the ears of corn next to Kotcininako's hips, as was the tradition. Kotcininako nursed the babies. The old woman placed water in a shell and rinsed it in her mouth before giving the boys water. The old woman brought Kotcininako fresh cornmeal to wash her body and yucca to wash her hair. The old woman took the life that follows, placed it in decorated bowls, and took them out to the river to bury.

The old woman then made a strengthening tea for Kotcininako. Together they sang a song of harmony. On the fourth day after the boys' birth, the old woman rose early and carried the boys out to introduce them to Sun, their father. The old woman then named the boys Masewi and Oyoyewi. Masewi was the Leader and Oyoyewi was the Follower.

Sun Father shone down on his sons. Tsityostinako examined the twins. She nodded in approval. The mother of these strong spirits had learned humility, honor, and spirit strength. Sun Father blessed his sons. He had sired these two for a reason. Masewi and Oyoyewi were brought into the world to control the people. Masewi would be the leader of the war chiefs, and Oyoyewi would be the protector.

6. Skeleton Boy

The Iroquois tell of a little nephew who lived with an old man in the dark woods. One day the old man went hunting, and just before leaving he told his nephew that he must not go eastward. The nephew played all morning and thought all the while about going in the forbidden direction. Finally, he decided to go to the east lake. He stopped and played. While he was playing, a man came to him and said, "Where do you come from, boy?" Then the man asked him if he would like to practice shooting arrows. The nephew liked the idea.

They shot their arrows up into the air. The nephew's arrow went higher than the man's. Then the man said, "Let us see who can swim farther without breathing." The nephew again beat the man. Then the man said, "Let us go to the island and look at the pretty birds." The nephew got into the man's canoe, which was pushed by three swans. As soon as they sat down in the canoe, the man began to sing a very loud song. Soon they arrived at an island. The man took off all the boy's clothes and said, "Come, let us swim to shore." The nephew jumped into the water and swam, following the man who sang while he swam.

The nephew pulled himself on shore. He looked around for the man but did not see him. The nephew wandered around calling for the man. Then he decided to look for the canoe and his clothes, but they were gone. The nephew sat on the shore and cried. He was lonely and cold. It grew dark very fast. The nephew sat and stared out in the darkness.

"Hsst! Keep still!"

The nephew looked around. He saw a skeleton on the ground near him. The skeleton said, "You have done what I did. Will you help me? I will help you."

The nephew agreed. The skeleton told him to go to a certain tree and dig on the west side of it. There the nephew would find a pipe, tobacco, and flint. The boy went to the tree and dug up the pipe, tobacco, and flint. The skeleton asked the nephew to fill the pipe and light it. The boy did.

"Put it in my mouth," said the skeleton.

The boy saw that mice filled the skeleton. He put the pipe into the skeleton's mouth, and the mice ran away. The skeleton then smiled and told the nephew that a man with three dogs was coming to the island that night to kill him. If the boy wanted to escape, he must run all over the island and jump into the water and out again so that the man would lose his trail. Then the boy should get into a hollow tree and stay there all night without moving.

The nephew did just that. In the early morning, he heard a canoe come ashore. He saw a man with three dogs. The man called to his dogs, "You must catch this animal." The man had the nephew's clothes. The dogs smelled the clothes and ran off. The man sat and waited on his canoe. The dogs returned. The man was angry that they had not found anyone. He killed one of the dogs and ate it right there.

The man took the other two dogs in his canoe and paddled back to the mainland. The nephew came out from his hiding place. He ran to the skeleton and the skeleton said, "Are you still alive?" The nephew said, "Yes."

The skeleton then said, "You must trick the man who brought you here. He will be arriving just before sunset. He will come to drink your blood. You must go down to the shore, bury yourself in the sand, hold very still, and wait for the man to get out of the canoe. He will search the island for you. When he is gone from the shore, you jump out of the sand, get into the canoe, and say, 'Swans, let's go home.' The swans will take you back to the mainland. Do not turn around, or it will be very bad. Look forward, and do not turn around. No matter what you hear, stare straight ahead."

The nephew hid in the sand, as he was told. Soon the man who had brought him came ashore on the island. The nephew jumped into the canoe and called to the swans. They went out into the water. The boy sang the song the man had sung. He had gone a distance in the water when he heard the man call out, "Come back, come back!"

The nephew did not look back. He came to a large rock with a hole. The swans went into the rock to a door. The nephew opened the door. When he entered the cave, he found his own clothes and the clothes of many others. He saw a fire and food all prepared, but no one was there. The boy put on his clothes and went to sleep.

In the morning, he found the fire and the food, but still there was no one. The nephew left the cave. The swans were still waiting. The nephew jumped into the canoe and said, "Come swans, let's go to the island." When he arrived, he found that the man who sucked blood had been killed and eaten up. The nephew ran to the skeleton.

The skeleton spoke to the boy, saying, "You are very smart. You can go and get your sister, whom this man carried off a long time ago. If you start tonight and go to the east, you will come to a very high rock where she goes for water. You will find her, and she will tell you what to do next."

The nephew started and in three days arrived at the rock. He found his sister. "Sister, come, let's go home," he said.

"No, I cannot," she answered. "A bad man keeps me here, and if he finds you he will kill you."

The nephew would not leave his sister.

This bad man had gone to a great swamp where women and children were picking cranberries. The sister went to the house, took up the plants over which her bed was made, and dug a pit underneath it for her brother. She hid her brother carefully so that he did not touch anything with his hands or his clothes. She covered him. She made her bed. She cooked a little food for her brother, and she put it with the wood by her bed. Then the sister lay down.

The bad man and his dogs returned. The dogs immediately began barking and running around. The man said, "Have you visitors?" She shook her head. The man said, "I know better." He had a long pole, and he poked at her with it.

She shook her head. "I have seen no one but you and dogs," she said. "You have food and you have water."

The man shook his head. "If I find anyone, I shall eat you for my morning meal."

In the morning, he started off for the swamp to gather some children for his dinner. He walked a bit and then decided to hide and watch the girl. As soon as the man was gone, she called to her brother, "Let us take the canoe and go quickly."

They ran and jumped into the canoe. But the man saw them and came after them, throwing a hook that caught the canoe. As he pulled it ashore, the line caught on a stone under the canoe and broke the hook. Brother and sister paddled very fast.

Now the man was enraged, and he lay down on the shore and began drinking water from the lake. The canoe started to return to the shore. As the man continued to drink, he grew very large with so much water. The nephew took a stone and threw it, hitting the man on the head so hard that it killed him. The water ran back into the lake, but now it was brown.

When they saw that the man was dead, they went back and the boy said to the two dogs, "You are very bad dogs. No one will want you now, so you are to go into the woods and be wolves."

The boy and his sister went to the island. The boy went to the skeleton. The skeleton said, "You are brave. You found your sister. Bring her to me." The nephew did this. Then the skeleton told them, "Gather up my bones and put them in a pile; then push the largest tree you see over on me and call out, 'All Dead People Arise.'" The nephew and his sister did this. And somehow the skeleton arose, and with it many others rose up out of the ground.

One had only one arm; one had only one leg; but they all had bows and arrows.

The nephew pulled his sister aside and said, "Come, we had better go home." When they arrived there, they found their uncle. He looked very tired and very old. For ten years he had cried at the loss of his little nephew. Now he was happy to have him home and with his niece.

The nephew told his uncle what had happened. The nephew said, "Let us build a new house for all of us." They did. The nephew went back to the island and brought all the people to live with them in their new house.

They learned of the healing of the dead. Those who are different hold healings that help us all. Many who are considered physically or mentally unusual can have special healings if they are observed and understood. Through our differences we learn who we are and what makes us whole.

7. Water-Jar Boy

This story was told by a very wise healer who called himself
Augustine Tenorio. He held the ability to heal in his words, and
this was his story of strength. "Healing comes from within, much
like the water jar," he would say. "We are not always strong.
Sometimes we need to hide until we are ready to see our way."
Healing is within each one of us. Each one of us needs healing;
healing alone or together, we can be healed whole.

A young woman noticed a young man playing his flute along
the river road as she walked to the river to gather water with the
other pueblo maidens. There were many flute players, but this
one young man had something special about him. The flute
player was a strong man with strength in his music. She followed
pueblo law and did not look at his face, especially his eyes, for
that was a commitment to marriage. Instead, she studied his
ankles and saw only pine and juniper boughs around them.

In the evening, when she returned to gather water from the
river for the morning wash, the strong man was there playing his
flute. She was impressed by his persistence. The young woman
asked her father about the strong man who played the flute. The
father asked the wise ones of the pueblo about the strong, young
man who played a certain tune on the flute and wore pine and
juniper on his ankles.

The wise ones said he was a good man, a strong man, one
who could provide, and one who was true in his heart. The father
asked if his daughter could have a union with the strong, young
man. The wise ones said no. The strong, young man was of a clan
that should not marry with the father's daughter. The water clans
should not marry into the hunting clans, at least not at this time.

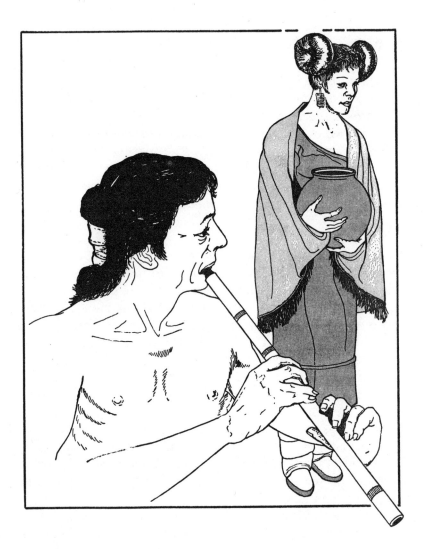

The father returned home and told his daughter. This maiden obeyed her father and the wise ones. She did not look at the strong, young man who played the flute every time she walked down to the river. The strong, young man persisted in his affection for her. She grew to respect his patience. The strong, young man asked if he could speak with the father of the maiden.

The wise ones said that they could not approve this union. The strong, young man asked if they could provide a testing for him to prove that, regardless of the clan, he would be good for his maiden. The wise ones spoke among themselves, asked the father for advice, and then asked the maiden. She agreed that a testing would be good, and if she tested as well, then they both would have the blessing of the wise ones. The testings began.

There were to be four testings. The first day the strong flute player was to gather wood enough for all the elders of the pueblo. The maiden was to sweep the plaza of the pueblo with pine branches. Even though both of them would be in the same area for some time during the day, they were not to communicate in any way. They did not speak to each other, never acknowledged the other, and saw nothing of the other's affection. They passed the first day's testing.

The second day's testing was harder. The strong flute player was sent out to find game animals and to track them, marking the trees for the hunters who were to follow the next day. The other strong, young men in the pueblo had gone out ahead and were leaving false animal paths, making animal noises, and trying to trick this strong man.

The young maiden was put to task with the washing of the elderly women's hair. She went out early and dug deeply in the desert soil to retrieve the yucca root to grind into a lather. This was then mixed with water, and after the elderly women's hair had been brushed, the young maiden washed their hair in the yucca and then plaited it as they wished. It was a very long day for both of them. They passed the testings.

The third day, the strong flute player was to go out in search of birds whose feathers could be used in the dances. He was to return with the bird feathers, leaving the birds free to fly. The bird feathers were to fill the pouch given to him by the wise ones.

The young maiden was to make corn bread. The people brought her their ears of corn, and she was to break off the kernels, grind them on a *metate* [grinding stone], using a *mano* [handstone]. This cornmeal was then to be soaked in fresh water, mixed with the ingredients given her, and baked in the outdoor *horno* [beehive-shaped, mud outdoor oven]. All this was to be done before dark. This was accomplished. They passed the testings.

The fourth day was one of patience. The two of them were to walk around the plaza in opposite directions four times to the beat of a drum. When the drum would stop, they were to walk four times in the other direction, doing this without looking at or noticing the other person in any way. This was done, and the wise ones had a meeting. All the testings had been passed by these two.

It was decided that on the morning of the fifth day, the young woman could wear her white *manta* [ceremonial dress] with the red and black fringe and walk from the east side of the plaza to meet the strong man. The strong flute player was to wear his embroidered kilt, white leggings, and brown moccasins. He would walk from the west and meet the maiden in the center of the plaza, and the union would then be official. This was done.

The wise ones suggested that they live away from the pueblo, for they did not want to encourage this kind of union. The young couple did as they were asked.

The young couple tried to have children. The babies born of the young woman were deformed, and before she could gather them up in her arms for prayer, birds flew from the sky and carried the deformed babies away. The young woman was very sad. The strong flute player turned his despair into hunting. He put all his energy into hunting, drying the meat, gathering pelts, and keeping his bows and arrows in excellent shape. They continued to hope for a baby that would be strong.

One morning the young woman went to the river to gather water. As she stood near the banks of the river, she called out to the spirits of the water. The spirits were known as *Pa'waa* [drowned spirits]. The young woman called to Pa'waa and told them of her wish to have a strong son. The Pa'waa heard her cries, and when she dipped the water jar into the river to gather water,

the water splashed onto her leg, and the spirit crawled up her leg and entered into her place of life replenishment. The spirits healed her and brought her life, letting the life grow quickly.

Within a moment she grew very fat with life. Her man was hunting, so she went to her mother's home in the pueblo. Her mother helped her secretly, for the young woman was not allowed to be in the pueblo. Soon she gave birth. Instead of a baby she birthed a round jar with two handles. It was a water jar. The water jar cried out for food. The woman pressed her breasts and filled another jar with fresh milk. The new grandmother poured the fresh breast milk into the opening of the birthed water jar's mouth.

The new mother was horrified, and she cried, and cried, and cried, and cried. The new grandfather asked the women to be patient, for this was magical.

The new mother took her water-jar child home, away from the pueblo. She put it in the corner of her home and waited for her man to return. He got home very late at night. As he entered and laid down his kill, he heard a small boy's voice calling out to him from the corner of the room. He walked over to the sound, lit a torch, and peered down at the water jar.

"Father, feed me, for I am hungry."

The strong man was amazed. He took some ground jerky meat and pushed it into the water jar. The boy's voice quieted down. The strong man thought this was most unusual.

Then the voice said, "Father, would you take me hunting with you tomorrow? I would like to learn what you know."

The strong man thought that this was good and promised to take the water-jar boy on the rabbit hunt the next day. The water-jar boy was quiet, and the strong flute player lay down with his woman.

In the morning, the strong flute player said that he was going to take the water-jar boy rabbit hunting. The new mother cried, and cried, and cried, and cried. She could not answer, for tears of sadness blocked her voice. The strong man took his water-jar son out on the hunt. The other hunters laughed at him. He did not notice them, for he was busy watching for the rabbits. The strong flute player pulled his rabbit stick from his belt, and when the

rabbits ran, he dropped the water-jar boy to throw his stick at the rabbits.

The water-jar boy rolled down the hill and hit hard against a rock. The flute player became fearful of what had happened to his water-jar son. Fear entered into the core of his being. The fear ate up his courage, his strength, and even ate up his bravery to live. The strong flute player fell on the ground, and life left his body. The strong flute player was now in another world.

The water jar broke, allowing a tall young man to emerge. The tall, young son wore white buckskin clothing, had long braided hair, and carried with him the spirit of ten men. The tall, young son aged quickly to be old enough to speak wisely, to run, and to tell when his life was in need. He ran to his father. He knelt down beside him and felt the absence of his father's life.

The tall young son knew that he must return home. The tall, young son carried his father almost to the house and then let him lie in the shade of a tall pine tree. The tall, young son went into the house and spoke with his mother.

"Mother, the strong man who was your man has gone to the other world. He dropped the water jar that held me, and in his fear he let the life pass out of him. I will take care of his body."

The young woman mother cried, and cried, and cried, and cried.

The tall, young son took his father and placed him in the rocks, facing east. The tall, young son went into the pueblo to meet with the people. They did not know him and were suspicious of him. The tall, young son asked about his father. No one knew where his father had come from; no one knew of his father's family; no one knew anything of his father. The tall, young son went home. He asked his mother about his father, but she cried, and cried, and cried, and cried, and could not speak because of her tears.

The tall, young son decided that he would go in search of his father's family, for they should know of their son and their grandson. The tall, young son walked to the east and found nothing. The tall, young son walked to the south and found nothing. The tall, young son walked to the west and found a natural spring pond. As the tall, young son bent down to drink of the fresh water, someone approached him.

"Are you searching for your father?" an older man asked him.

"Yes, do you know of him?" the tall, young son answered.

"Would you know him if you saw him?" the older man responded.

"You are he, are you not?" replied the tall, young son. The father took his tall, young son with him to the opening in the spring pond. They entered into the spring pond, and with the water rushing over them, they were submerged under the water. They moved with little effort, and they went round and round, round and round, until they crossed a bridge to another place. This was the place of the Pa'waa.

The strong father taught his tall, young son of life under the water. They had a good life. Then the tall, young son asked about his mother. The strong father could not answer, for he was not allowed to speak of those who were not there in that place.

The tall, young son decided to go back to his mother and tell her of her man. The tall, young son made the journey back alone, and when he returned to the pueblo, he found his mother very ill. She cried, and cried, and cried, and cried. She had very little food and would not eat. She would not listen to her son but cried, and cried, and cried, and cried. The people in the pueblo ignored the tall, young son, for they had thought that he had abandoned his young woman mother. The young woman mother let the life spirit leave her body, and she was no longer in this place.

The tall, young son prayed for his mother to move on to the other place. He did as taught by the spirits, for none of the pueblo people would talk to him. After four days the tall, young son decided that there was nothing there to keep him at his home. He took very little and found his way back to the spring pond. He entered the place of the Pa'waa where his father lived.

When he arrived he found his young woman mother there. The three of them lived there for as long as Augustine knew, for there was plenty of food and shelter, and there were stories to keep them until the spirits decided otherwise.

Augustine died in 1992, but his story is still here. May this story heal you.

Story Notes

Cherokee Dreams of Respect

When all of life spoke the same language, there was much happening everywhere. This day was filled with laughter, sacred smoke, and the exchange of spirit energy. Ramos Greyhorse had come in first in the horse race around the mesa. The ravens were flying high and the winds were slow and lazy high up. Men's voices echoed their laughter as the children played down below the overhang in the shade. Women were busy in the kitchens, sharing family news and cooking. Ramos Greyhorse tossed his grandfather his sweat-filled, red bandanna, and I caught it. Grandpa Greyhorse watched his grandson jerk the horse around and head off to the north canyon. "He's going to meet his woman. He's proud and she's waiting for him." He lifted his chin in the air to the east. "He needs to treat the horse with respect. Animals remember the old ones' ways and meetings." Grandpa Greyhorse then told me this story.

Cedar Tree Medicine

Yuchi people knew of evil ways. Yuchi dancers danced to keep the evil away. Tall pine talked in the summer wind as drums beat to talking feet dancing at the Squaw Dance. Fried bread dripped grease as the rodeo men laughed, talked, passed the bottle. Old men eyed the young squaws readying to dance. The women talked of men and the color of the cedar trees that talked with the drum. They told this story.

Hozin'i Chant

"Navaho visions, visions of people, visions held in the head, guide the body to a place of balance." Rosemary Trujillo smiled at me. I let her stroke my hair. We were on a blanket under a tall cottonwood tree. "If you are to be a healer, then you need to know of visions. Visions take you to places that are not safe; they are not places where your logical mind would ever let you go. They are places that you *need* to go. Much has happened in everyone's life. Much needs to be released. To release this pain, struggle, hope, fear, inner path, one needs to travel in a vision."

Her hands pulled me. I lay down with my head in her lap, my body stretched out in front of her. "This is the birthing position and I will hold you, guide you, love you, and be with you on this vision."

The Navaho-Hozin'i chant takes the vision seeker on a path of beauty, but not without pain, fear, courage, and love. Love must engulf the vision seeker or the vision will not be true. Rosemary will tell you this; she will hold you and guide you with her love.

Kiowa Medicine House

Taime, sacred bundle, sacred way of the people is still sacred. Kiowa travel this country, nurturing the land and are hope-filled for a home that they can call their own. They have been displaced over and over again. Oklahoma holds many Kiowa. Yet, they move on, seeking a place where they can be held by the land and feel that it is home. Many Kiowa live here in New Mexico. We share communities, schools, dreams, and roadways. Carol Smithey told this story of the *taime.* "The Kiowa," she said, "always find a way to get what they need, whether it is shared, given, or taken back. Kiowa keep strong."

Buffalo-Dung Boy

Blackfeet folks love the pow-wow. And, of course, so do we. My daughters sit and watch until it is time for them to be involved. Then they either hide or jump right in. There was a time when they chose to hide. The dance floor was filled, the drums were very loud next to the microphone, and they said they didn't feel like getting "into it."

They hid in the women's bathroom. A grandmother with long, dark hair down to the back of her knees was wrapping up the *pa'hoos* [prayer sticks] from her dance in a piece of white buckskin. She noticed the girls hiding. When I came in search of them, she smiled at me and jerked her chin toward the far bathroom stall.

"They are being the Buffalo-Dung girls." She smiled as she spoke with a very stern voice. "They do not want to be seen, but they want to be helpful." She opened her folding chair, lifted her small suitcase onto her lap, and as she folded her costume in the suitcase, she told us the story of the Buffalo-Dung Boy. The girls came out, but they did not participate in the pow-wow.

Ani-Kuta-ni

Cherokee healers are known for their power of myth and magic. Both work well, as this story illustrates. This story was told to me by Charlie Runninghorse at the Oklahoma State Fair.

Uktena

Uktena is told with great reverence. Paul Vargas and his woman Jule stood in the one-hundred-year-old adobe home. His dark brown eyes glistened. His strong New Mexican Indian hand held his wife's hand. This story of the old ones tells of hope, desire, and a better life. "Isn't that what we are all still searching for?" Paul asked. There is always hope, still there is always hope.

Dasi-giya-gi

Dark Night Sky hid our faces from Wise One with the drum. His voice echoed down passages of our souls as we desperately tried to see his face through the black. He stopped his drum the second night of four-night-healing tellings. His story pounded from the belly of a drum, startling bright-light visions rattling through our heads, healing with thunder words stories from the old ones.

Delaware Hunter

"Bear clan's eldest member died on October 10, 1951." The bus rolled down the hot, black pavement to Gallup. "He was the strong one and knew all the stories. We only remember the faces; few of us remember the stories. But, maybe you might like this story. I learned it from the old one." Grizzled grey-green eyes grinned at me from the window seat. "Would you like to hear a story?"

"Of course, you know I would."

Male Healing

Teaching creative writing and storytelling at the Bernalillo Middle School brought about a different perspective on life. Nancy Noble's English class pushed me to the limit. They asked me to tell them their creation myths, their reasons for speaking rather than writing. One student waited until I finished the Keres creation myth, stood, nodded in respect, and then told his version. Here it is. Thank you, Nancy Noble.

Creation and Emergence

Tanoan stories started at the beginning of time. This oral narration is traditional. It is taught to ankle biters and known by the old ones.

This story comes from the inner core of knowing before one knows.
This story comes from the beginning and is told to bring harmony.

Ololowishka

Bertha Dutton is the leading living female ethnologist in the United
States. She worked on the Kuaua site, also known as Coronado's
Monument. There is a kiva there that held several layers of murals.
She found a way to remove the layers, document the murals, and
leave the kiva intact. We worked together in 1986 to reconstruct the
pictographs and their myths. This was one of the paintings or
pictographs. You can still see it today at Kuaua. The ceremony is still
done for perpetuation of life.

Macta-hotcanyi

Stevie Mac, friend and teacher, visited the Blessing Way with me
several years back. She was interested in the clans, the designation
of order, division of duties, et al. When we stopped at a friend's
house in Galisteo to get tamales for lunch, this was how the war
chiefs were defined to us.

Sacred Sisters

Alex Apostolides, Patti Apostolides, Bud Hampton, Alec Patterson,
Mary Patterson, Richard Silverstein, and many more were curious as
to the story behind this old and sacred pictograph panel. The Bureau
of Land Management, who owned this panel, held very little interest
in it. These folks took a group of tellers up to the panel, and engraved
there was the famous old, old, old, old story of the Sacred Sisters.
The Birth of War is one of the oldest stories in the Keres and the
Tanoan language groups. The story is still there; the story is also
here, and now you can tell it.

Raven

The post office closed at four-thirty in the afternoon. I pulled on the
door, but it was locked. A man sitting under the portal nodded to
me. "It's closed. It will be closed until tomorrow."

I studied his face. He appeared to be firm in his location. "Are you
waiting until tomorrow?"

He nodded.

"Do you live around here?"

He shook his head.

"Do you have a story?"

He nodded.

We fixed a fine dinner that night. He was a healer with the Kak
Clan or Raven Clan. He told the girls and me his story. It is a fine
story.

Maple Syrup and Menstruation

Aunt Rose Rainbow had been a healer in the Midwest. Aunt Rose Rainbow lives at the edge of Tuba City. No one knows where she came from, and no one knows where she goes in the winter. She'd come into town, stand at the door of the fried chicken store, and nod as the people went in and out. Her gestures appeared to be of duty.

After a day of research, we went to the fried chicken store. There she was, nodding and nodding. She made all feel good as they were going in and out of the store. Our research, repelling-crew captain Jeremy Davis pulled open the door and would not go in until Aunt Rose Rainbow went in. Aunt Rose Rainbow blushed, walked in, and started back out again.

Jeremy Davis grabbed her arm, sat her in a booth, and proceeded to get her a full basket of fried chicken and fries. She ate quickly, told us this story, wiped off her wrinkled face, hurried outside, and proceeded to nod at the folks coming and going. Bet she's there right now.

The Old Children

"Flintnapper, horsetheiver, rattlesnake catcher, bull rider, tobacco spitter, and womanizer. Yup, I be all those things, but I never married a woman that wasn't right for me at the time." Silver Rabbit Blazer spat. His forty-four-year-old tanned face beamed as he spoke. His first healing had been performed, and his first patient was walking and feeling pretty good.

"Yup, you gotta watch out for the way you feel towards a woman." He spat out of the corner of his mouth. "This here is the story I learned about such things. It has a healing to itself, this story does; if you listen to each word, you'll know what I'm saying."

Here is Silver Rabbit Blazer's healing story.

Chants

These chants were collected over the years from different ceremonies that I attended or participated in. They do have certain people behind them whom I respect and who wish to remain unknown. Enjoy the chants, chant them, and find harmony.

Tusayan Walpi

"Did you know that if you stuck a spear through the globe starting at Oraibi, Hopi, it would come out at Nepal?"

"No, I had no idea."

"Did you know that everyone came out of the center of the earth, and the Spirit of the Feeling World, Myuingwa, with Baholikonga serpent, brought everyone here?"

"No, I did not know that."

"Well, if you keep washing the dishes, and if you keep quiet, I will tell you more than you want to know."

Mountain Way

Life is not always easy. At times while we gather at tellings, healings, or shopping, other people's problems become obvious. This story was told to me at the grocery store at Puray, New Mexico by a woman who was waiting for her disability check. I bought her a Pueblo sandwich and she told me a story.

Black Turtle Chant

Years ago, I told stories at the Palace of the Governors in Santa Fe. A beautiful patio with nice shade trees, folding chairs, and a soft, cool breeze kept the tellings peaceful and pleasant. One afternoon I had just finished a telling when a grandmother and her three grandsons came and sat down. The grandmother told this story to her grandsons as she pointed to the sun overhead. She smiled at me. I smiled back. It was a good day.

Palyatuma's First Commandments

This chant is a known only among the Hopi and Pueblo people.

Noko'mis of the Menomini

Sergio F. Manriquez and Marilyn Feathers invited me to Shiwi, or Zuni Middle School, to share stories. Sergio's family is Nahuatl, and Marilyn's family is Pawnee. When I arrived the students were Zuni, some Hopi, and a couple of mixed bloods. We shared stories and had a great time. A substitute teacher, whose name I don't think I ever heard, told me this story as we waited for the basketball game to begin. He said, "The words, the sounds of the words, the way the words flow, these heal and bring inner peace. This story should always be an out-loud story, for it brings balance from the words."

Earth Magician Vision

Henrietta Stockel knows of the Apache ways. She has written, lived with, and done ceremony with the Apache people. When I was asked to do research at Lipan Apache area, I asked her about the ways of the people. She said, "Talk to the people. Ask them yourself." Being raised in the Pueblo, I was not eager to talk to the Apache. The Apache helped me and their kindness is greatly appreciated, as is this story that comes from the Apache way.

Cherokee Healing

David Alcoze is Cherokee, not Cheyenne. Jennifer and Chuck Couch made that very clear. They also went with me to Hopi, where we met another Cherokee. She told us this story while we waited in line at the Hopi Convention Center for the store to open. As she talked, her hand weaved the story. Her eyes held great beauty.

Absonnutli

Sheepherding takes endurance and the Teec Nos Pos Trading Post has the coldest drinks. Teec Nos Pos is on the four-corners area and is an oasis for all travelers. Cold orange soda with a bag of crisp potato chips helps keep the heat of summer down and the mood hospitable. These Navaho stories were told here, over a period of four summers of sheepherding. Gathering the sheep also brings together the sheepherders and all their stories. The sheep are healing, the land is peaceful, and the stories repeat over and over in your mind as you solitarily herd your sheep across the silent folds of brown Earth Woman.

Hasjelti and Hostjoghon

Lauren Elizabeth Geismar read me this story. She is nine years old. The power of the story and the beauty of the mountains dressed in shells, turquoise, and eagle plumes came to life in her voice and eyes. This story is from the old, old Navaho and is still very much alive today.

Naiyenesgony and Tobaidischinni

Denise O'Connor walked along the path of the Blessing Way. She studied the ground as the old stories were told to us. The wind blew softly letting it cool our bodies in the heat of the summer. "It is time to know that all people are one. It is time to appreciate one another. Each person feels, each person sees life through different eyes; the perceptions of the stories is different, each taking from the story what they need."

Ravens flew overhead. The feathers of the grandmothers were tied in their long braids. Denise glanced at me. Her eyes spoke of her love for the land, life. Beauty radiated from her.

Wind Mountain Brothers

Ryan Geismar, Tanya Russ, John Spang, Mary Diane Hausman, Kirk and Susan Hauptman, June Sevilla, Margie Ann Stanko, Monelle Holley, Susan Baugh, Al and Mary Geismar, Julie McAvity, Oliver and Janna Pijoan, Janet Shaw, and a handful of young folks have all graced the cliff face of Comanche Gap and know the writing of the ancient ones. The story of the Wind Mountain Brothers is here from the Navaho People. The loyalty of brothers, the beauty of family, and the warmth of the mountain have brought us all together. Here is the story of the Wind Mountain Brothers.

Healers on the Mountain

Alessandro B. Salimbeni asked about life. The life of the Raven Caller had disappeared from the valley. Alessandro asked about healing. Alessandro wanted to know about the old ways, the ways of the people here in this place. That night I went to a gathering. When I mentioned Alessandro's question, the old ones said, "Tell him this story. Tell him of the Healers on the Mountain." Here, then, Alessandro B. Salimbeni, is the story of the healers.

Guiana Medicine and the Crows

Two of us sat in the back of the battered, old grey pickup. Both of us were without vehicles that functioned. His dark brown eyes met mine; mine were brown as well. His dark-brown skin was darker than mine. He smiled, showing me some of his filled teeth. I nodded. After forty minutes of silence, he spoke about life in Guiana. His accent complemented his stories. He said that to understand a story one must hear it—not read it, but hear it—out loud. To hear the story not only enables the listener to understand the story, but allows the story to heal the listener. I nodded. He told this story.

Guiana Healers

The co-rider in the back of the pickup got out in Socorro, New Mexico. I got out as well. There were still many miles to go and the gas station was a nice release from the noisy, bouncing truck. We got a soda and a candy bar, leaned against the hot, cinderblock garage wall, and shared more stories. I learned that his name was Gregory Allen, but he liked to be called Orie.

Wolverine's Sister

Pow-wow time in Alguguerque brings all kinds of fascinating folks. The beauty of the costumes illuminates the faces that hold many stories. Grandfather Running Bear from Oklahoma told four of us this story. He then gave each of us a deerskin necklace of horsemint.

Thunder Being

"Wish I had a Thunder Being." A grandfather turned to me. His bandanna was sweat-laden, his hands were grizzled and calloused. "I have missed my breakfast standing in this line." He waved with his other hand and softly hit my chest. "It is a good thing we are poor." He pointed to the banktellers counting out the satchels of money. "They aren't going to get lunch either; they will be lucky to eat dinner." He swung his hand around and hit me on the other side of my chest. I went concave.

"Thunder Being would bellow and let us poor people get our business done so we could get back to work. Look, it is our money that they are counting." He swung to hit me in the chest again, but

I backed away in a second. He smiled. "Do you want to hear about the Thunder Being while we wait for lunch?" I stepped back and smiled.

Arapaho Woman and the Butterflies

Nicole poked Denise O'Connor in the ribs. "Look at the black butterflies. Do you know about the black butterflies?" Denise shook her head. Nicole frowned. "You must know about the black butterflies!"

Denise shook her head. "I am from New York; I wouldn't know a black butterfly."

Nicole's eyes smiled. The story unfolded.

Kotcininako

This is one of the oldest Keres and Tanoan myths. Children are told this story almost as soon as they can talk. The power of the twins, the power of belief, the power of trust and wholeness come alive in this great fine myth.

Skeleton Boy

Eleanor Ott and Hannelore Hahn took me under their wings when I went to New York City. It was as foreigh a place as I ever want to go again. As I wandered the city trying to find the tree reservation and some dirt, I met another wanderer, an Iroquois healer. I told him of my discomfort in this big city and he told me this story. I did not complain again.

Water -Jar Boy

Augustine Tenorio was the finest healer I ever knew. He could heal with his eyes, a smile, a wave of his hand. Magic clung to his spirit and he made the world around him whole. To be in his company was profound. To be taught by him was to know beyond what there is to know. Burned, battered, beaten, weathered, worn, wounded, cut, crazed, or starved, Augustine would heal. Augustine loved popcorn and cold coffee with milk. This is his story out of love for him, for he is missed.